THE
Winning
FORMULA

Discover how to live a life of possibility!

FATAI KASALI

THE **WINNING** FORMULA

Published in the United Kingdom by Glory Publishing

ISBN: 978-0-9926138-3-9

Acknowledgements

To God be the glory for the grace to write this book. I give God all the praise and adoration for giving me the inspiration through His Spirit. This has made possible the writing of this book.

My sincere thanks go to Mr Adeyemi Bukola for his diverse support and contribution during the period of editing this book. I am indeed very grateful. May God almighty send you help in all your ways in Jesus name.

My wife, Felicia Ebunlomo, gave me priceless support during the writing of this book. I thank God almighty for giving me such a wonderful wife. My two sons, David and Daniel, have been very supportive. May God almighty bless you all.

Introduction

Life is a battle. It is full of different kind of challenges. It does not matter who you are and where you live, there will always be something to contend with in life. The world we live in is full of confrontation and attack. They come in different ways and manners. Some of these challenging situations are spiritual, while others are physical.

It is never totally quiet in life. There are noises here and there. Some are real while others are imaginary. Our minds are under constant bombardment from activities originated from both fellow human beings and spiritual forces.

Ephesians 6:12
For we wrestle not against flesh and blood, but against principalities, against powers, against the rulers of the darkness of this world, against spiritual wickedness in high places.

Indeed, life is full of different kind of things we have to wrestle with. We wrestle because we have to refuse to surrender to the dictate of evil forces. We wrestle because we have to refuse to live a life of defeat. Unless we wrestle until victory comes, our lives maybe full of defeat and frustration. To those that refuse to surrender to the dictate of evil forces, divine help shall be made available to win. You can only win in life if you refuse to surrender. You can only win in life if you take your stand against oppression and dictate of negative forces. These negative forces manifest through human vessels to make life of innocent people miserable. Also, they can choose to operate alone if permitted by their victims. There are so many lives demonic forces have destroyed just because their victims did not rise against them.

This book will educate you about how to work out victory in the battles of life. You will learn in this book how to live a life that wins. The winning formula is about what to do to win the battles of life. You will learn how Moses defeated Pharaoh despite series of frustrations he faced. This case will motivate you not to surrender to the enemy irrespective of the level of threat and intimidation. With God on your side, you can overcome any challenge. With God on your side, you do not need to consider the possibility of defeat in any of your battles. You were created and born to win in life. God wants you to win because that will glorify His name in your life.

I pray that as you read this book, the Spirit of the most High God will illuminate your mind and strengthen you to win always. Amen.

Contents

- 1 -

The Battles of Life

Life is about battles. It is a place where you have to fight for everything in order to have it. And after you have it, you will still need to continue fighting in order to keep it, because there are thieves who want to steal what you have.

Those who reign in life are those who perpetually win the battles of life. But what kind of battles are we talking about? Not guns and bullets or swords and shields, obviously. But we are all involved in struggles to overcome some kind of opposition – an enemy. The battles of life involve contending against hindrances – both physical and spiritual. And what are the battles for? They are to improve your life. There are many obstacles to success, many barriers to overcome, if we want to possess what is really valuable in life.

THE REALITY OF BATTLES

The battles of life are real and there is no escape from them. You will need to get ready for war, otherwise you will never reign in life.

Deuteronomy 2:24 says: *"Rise ye up, take your journey, and pass over the river Arnon: behold, I have given into thine hand Sihon the Amorite, king of Heshbon, and his land: begin to possess it, and contend with him in battle."*

In this verse God told the Israelites that He had given them the land to possess, but they still needed to fight in order to make it a reality. They needed to overcome the illegal occupiers of the land.

You must understand that your enemies have gone ahead of you before you were born, and have taken possession of what God gave you before the creation of the earth. You will need to contend with illegal occupiers that have taken possession of what belongs to you. You must realise that there are barriers to the blessings intended for you, and unless you are ready for battle, you will not be able to claim those blessings. Sometimes the devil brings somebody to steal the position that God gave you before the creation of this world. To reclaim it you will have to fight for it.

John 16:33 says: *"These things I have spoken unto you, that in me ye might have peace. In the world ye shall have tribulation: but be of good cheer; I have overcome the world."*

Here Jesus shared the reality of what the future holds for all disciples – in every age. He told his disciples to prepare for battle. This is because the forces of darkness will always be at war with the army of light. The reality of this life is that there is 'tribulation' – trouble – everywhere in the world. The children of God encounter more of this tribulation if they continually refuse to compromise their salvation, and to reject what the world throws at them. You need to get ready for battle if you want to stay on God's side and please Him always.

The battle is real but, praise God, the victory is also certain! As Jesus said, *"In the world ye shall have tribulation: but be of good* cheer; I have overcome the world" *(John 16:33)*. We are on the winning side!

1 Timothy 6:12 says: *"Fight the good fight of faith, lay hold on eternal life, whereunto thou art also called, and hast professed a good profession before many witnesses."*

Faith in the Lord requires a fight because there are things the enemy will throw in your way to defeat your faith. You will need to enter the fray and be determined not to surrender. God wants you to always resist the devil until he flees from you *(James 4:7)*.

ORIGIN OF THE WAR

Revelation 12:7-10

"And there was war in heaven: Michael and his angels fought against the dragon; and the dragon fought and his angels, and prevailed not; neither was their place found any more in heaven. And the great dragon was cast out, that old serpent, called the Devil, and Satan, which deceiveth the whole world: he was cast out into the earth, and his angels were cast out with him. And I heard a loud voice saying in heaven, Now is come salvation, and strength, and the kingdom of our God, and the power of his Christ: for the accuser of our brethren is cast down, which accused them before our God day and night."

There once was a war in heaven. The angels of God fought against the devil and all his hosts. Satan had rebelled against God and created division among the angels in heaven – those who sided with the devil and those who were faithful to God. God's angels won and the devil and his angels (who turned into demons) were cast out of heaven.

The devil is the origin of all confusion. Wherever the devil is there will always be conflict. Since the day the devil entered into this world, men have never experienced perfect peace. People are turned against each other. There is conflict and suspicion everywhere.

Nations fight against nations, tribes against tribes, and religions against religions. Businesses are destroyed by false accusations from outside and strife within. Human beings are turned into vessels of destruction in the hand of the devil. Members of the same family are turned against each other. Marriages are under incessant threat because of disputes and disagreement. Even some churches are split by rows, disunity and conflicts.

All are the works of the devil. When the devil is allowed in a place he creates battles for people to fight. When he is allowed inside a person, he creates battles within the person. The devil can turn a man against himself, until he unwittingly destroys himself. The devil loves to make simple things complicated – he's an expert at that! He can enter into a person to make him a hindrance to another man's journey. You can trace every evil done in this world back to the devil. Where he can't operate alone, he seeks a human agent to possess or influence, to use against a fellow human being.

Although everyone is responsible for their own sin, the devil is the tempter who attracts people to sin. That is why I say every evil is traced back to him.

Ephesians 6:12 says: *"For we wrestle not against flesh and blood, but against principalities, against powers, against the rulers of the darkness of this world, against spiritual wickedness in high places."*

Your real enemy to fight is the devil. He is the one who creates hatred, complication and every manner of confusion. He is the one that makes men hate men. He is the one who invades a good system to corrupt it. If allowed, he can turn a peaceable home into a war zone. He exploits individual weaknesses to create arguments that will lead to confusion and strife. That is why you will never be a winner in life if you focus on human agents and ignore the devil. Every evil you have experienced from man can be traced back to the devil. He is behind every evil done.

In **Genesis 3**, Adam and Eve never had any problem in their relationship until the devil entered the Garden to tempt them. He craftily and subtly turned them against each other and against God. The same still holds true today. We are all infected with the devil's disease of rebellion against God, and deceitfulness of heart **(Jeremiah 17:9)**.

Since the fall of humanity, the devil has always been able to create friction in the human community. He exploits our weaknesses to lure us into conflict. That is why you must know that your real enemy to fight throughout your days on earth is no other person but the devil. Your enemy is not your manager that hates you, nor your in-laws who undermine you, nor your neighbours who gossip about you. You must love them all. It is the devil that keeps on exploiting the weaknesses in men to turn them against each other, and you must do battle with him and his demons. Simple things become complicated when the devil is involved.

2 Corinthians 10:4 says: *"For the weapons of our warfare are not carnal, but mighty through God to the pulling down of strong holds..."*

Our weapons are not carnal – physical – but spiritual, because the enemy we are fighting is not made of flesh and blood but of the spirit. You will always win if you direct your attention to the devil, not human beings. Man is just an instrument that he uses. As long as you live among other human beings there will always be a battle to fight!

People don't need to know you before they rise against you. The devil knows that they carry his evil seed inside of them, so he manipulates them to rise against you. It is the devil that attacks your own mind with a series of evil thoughts and imaginations. He attacks your mind to make you a loser. He lies to you to make you follow the wrong path in life.

The devil is a schemer. He has devices and strategies. He uses men against each other. He creates enmity and he is the author of confusion. He knows how to turn a husband against his wife and vice-versa. If he is allowed to work, he can do unimaginable damage. That is why you must make the devil your focus, not human beings. You must engage him in battle using spiritual weapons. Our weapons include prayer, the name of Jesus, the blood of Jesus, the word of God and the word of our testimony. None of these is carnal. They are spiritual weapons meant to fight the spiritual forces of hell. They are not meant to fight human beings but the devil and his powers.

TYPES OF BATTLES

The battles of life can be divided into two separate groups, which are:

1 – The inner battles

These are battles that take place inside of a man.

> ### Galatians 5:17
> *"For the flesh lusteth against the Spirit, and the Spirit against the flesh: and these are contrary the one to the other: so that ye cannot do the things that ye would."*

The spirit and flesh fight against each other within us. When we lose this battle we do things we don't want to do. The one that captures us will begin to dictate to us what to do and what not to do. The flesh does not want to surrender to the dictates of the Spirit of God who lives inside us. So the flesh becomes a hindrance that needs to be defeated. Unless it is defeated, it will exercise dominion over our thinking pattern and dictate our actions. The devil will gain access into our lives if we allow our flesh to compromise our faith.

Once the devil succeeds in gaining the support of our flesh, the two will begin to work in partnership to lead us away from God. They will resist every good desire the Spirit of God brings into us, and they will establish their own desires.

We must acknowledge the fact that there is a constant battle going on inside of us. The devil is externally communicating to your flesh inside of you, to gain control of your soul. This is a battle you must fight and win – otherwise, you will lose your soul.

Signs that you are losing the inner battle are:

A. Worldly desires

Romans 8:5
"For they that are after the flesh do mind the things of the flesh; but they that are after the Spirit the things of the Spirit."

You are losing the inner battle when you begin to focus on things of the flesh. When you begin to see no wrong in things that don't glorify the name of God, then you are losing the inner battle. When you become liberal about those things God has declared wrong, then you are being defeated in the internal war. When you develop more interest in things that don't benefit your spirit than things that do, you are failing in the inward fight. When you try to justify and give reasonable excuses for disobedience to God, you are surrendering to the enemy.

B.   Slavery to sin

Romans 7:19
"For the good that I would I do not: but the evil which I would not, that I do."

You are losing the inner spiritual battle if you find yourself doing things you know to be wrong, unintentionally. This implies that the flesh has taken over and is succeeding in silencing the Spirit of God who lives in you. It implies that you have lost resistance to the power of the flesh. You have become Mister or Sister 'Yes, Sir' to the flesh; whatever the flesh asks you to do, you will do even against your own heart's desire or the will of your mind.

This usually comes with regret and sorrow of the heart. You feel remorse about doing the wrong that you did. Unfortunately, you will see yourself doing the same wrong thing next time. It is because the flesh has taken over. Wrong things become demonic when they turn into habits and addiction; that is, you can no longer do without committing the wrong habit. It becomes a way of life for you. It implies that hell has sent a certain demon to work with your flesh to take you deeper into the wrong habits. When you notice this kind of situation in your life, seek deliverance, and attack the enemy with intense prayer and fasting. You may also need to ask a trusted Christian leader or friend to pray with you.

C. Insensitivity

> ### Jeremiah 5:21
> *"Hear now this, O foolish people, and without understanding; which have eyes, and see not; which have ears, and hear not."*

You are losing the inner battle if you notice that you can no longer perceive God's spiritual touch. When the flesh succeeds in taking over your soul, the first thing it will do in collaboration with the devil is to blind the eyes of the mind and block the inner ears. This hinders you from being able to receive spiritual signals from God. At this stage, you no longer have heavenly vision and dreams. All your vision and dreams will start coming from the flesh and the hosts of hell. When you begin to feel as if God is far away from you, it may be that your flesh has won you over. It is time for spiritual restoration and renewal.

D. Loss of the joy of salvation

> ### Psalm 51:12
> *"Restore unto me the joy of thy salvation; and uphold me with thy free spirit."*

You are losing the inner battle if you notice that you have lost the joy of being saved. There is a deep joy in knowing God and having a relationship with Him. When this is no longer your experience, or when it no longer excites you, then you are being defeated inside. The joy of salvation can only be maintained in your life by the presence of the Holy Spirit, but when the flesh succeeds in taking over your soul, the influence of the Spirit of God will be hindered and eroded. When there is a loss of joy, the following set in: fear, anxiety, demotivation, discouragement, worry, evil imagination, stress, etc.

E.   Walking in your own counsel

> *Psalm 81:12*
> *"So I gave them up unto their own hearts' lust: and they walked in their own counsels."*

You are losing the inner battle when you begin to listen to your own desires and see your own decisions as better than God's instructions. You no longer consult God before you do anything. You no longer acknowledge God in your ways. Your ideas appear better. When the flesh succeeds in winning you over, it will work with the devil to separate you from God. You will notice that you feel comfortable doing things without seeking the face of God. When this becomes your experience, then you must realise that the flesh has taken over your soul. It is time to wake up and fight your way back to the Lord.

2 – The outer battles

These battles take place outside of you. They originate from things the world and the hosts of hell throw at you as you daily live your life.

Let's consider some examples of those things you may need to fight for in life.

A. Your possessions

2 Chronicles 20:11
"Behold, I say, how they reward us, to come to cast us out
of thy possession, which thou hast given us to inherit."

Possessions are such things as money, job, career, educational attainment, and everything that God has given you to live a God-glorifying life. Some of your possessions are in the hands of another man and you will need to fight (spiritually) for them. Some of your possessions are locked up in a particular office and you may need to fight (spiritually) to access them.

For example, you may need to attend an interview to get a certain job, and the interview may be very tough, but unless you pass, you will not be given the job. It may also be that there are many competitors for the same job. You will need to get ready to fight your way through.

Also, a position of honour is your inheritance but you may need to fight for it. In **Esther 2**, Esther had to compete with many virgins in the land to become the queen. She refused to allow her poor social status to intimidate her, and she won. Health and healing is your possession, but at times you may need to fight for it. In **Mark 5**, a woman with a blood haemorrhage kept on fighting for her health until she won. For 12 years she was sick, but despite the frustration she kept on seeking a solution and one day she found it. She was made whole by Jesus. Even on the day of her miracle she had to fight a large crowd that would not let her touch Jesus. She refused to accept that seeing Jesus was impossible due to the large crowd. She found her way round it and got her healing.

Long life is your possession because God has promised it, but sometimes you may need to fight for it. In Isaiah 38, Hezekiah had to fight for his life. He was "sick unto death" (verse one) but he refused to accept it. God extended his life by 15 years because Hezekiah refused to die prematurely. He wanted more years to complete the good work of restoration he was doing for God. When you receive the report of death, it will be your responsibility to reject it. When you are told that your sickness is incurable, it will be your responsibility to refuse and reject such a report. If you refuse and reject it, you will live longer. As the devil continues to attack your mind, making you think that you will die as the experts have said, you will need to fight that evil thought and imagination.

Recovery is your possession, but you may need to fight for it.

It will not be cheap to recover all your losses. In 1 Samuel 30, David had to fight to recover what the enemy had stolen from his life. He consulted God before he launched out, and God directed his steps. You can recover all the enemy has stolen from your life if you can do what David did – refuse to cry over your losses, but instead rise up against them. God has promised you in his word blessings that are real and yours, but you will need to chase them and if necessary, fight to possess them. Furthermore, after you have fought to possess your possession, you may need to fight again in order to keep it yours. This is because there are thieves that come to steal and destroy.

For example, in *2 Chronicles 20*, Moabites, Ammonites and some Moabites came to attack Jehoshaphat to take over the land God had given to Judah. The people cried to God and He delivered them. They fought the enemy through praising God and refusal to surrender their inheritance. There are people who want to steal your blessings; you must not surrender your inheritance but resist them until you win.

B. Your marriage

To keep your home from the attack of home destroyers, you will need to fight until you win. Hell has set forces in motion to destroy your marriage and you will need to engage them in battle.

In *1 Samuel 1*, Hannah was the first wife of her husband, Elkanah, but due to barrenness, he married a second wife, Peninnah. Hannah refused to leave Elkanah and refused to surrender to Peninnah's mockery and taunts. Because Hannah refused to surrender, and appealed to God in prayer, God fought for her. If you refuse to surrender in whatever battle you face, and take it to the Lord in prayer, God will fight on your side. Your endurance and faith will provoke divine involvement.

Whatever comes against your marriage, you need to resist, then, God will get involved on your behalf. It may be the threat of divorce, financial difficulty, or the interference of in-laws, etc. But if you can focus on your God in all that the enemy is throwing at your marriage, soon, you will win.

C. Your dreams and vision

The fulfilment of your dreams and vision will not come easy. You will need to fight for them. There are forces of hell that operate through human elements to frustrate good dreams and vision. You will need to resist their attack and refuse to surrender your vision and dreams. There are many ways that your enemy seeks to destroy the vision and dreams that God has laid on your heart. The devil's attack could manifest through financial hardship.

Severe financial insufficiency may threaten your ministry or plans, but you must refuse to surrender. Demonic spirits could operate through envious people, raising them up against you to try to force you to give in.

In the story of Nehemiah, all the dream killers the devil raised against Nehemiah failed. Nehemiah celebrated the completion of his vision because he refused to surrender to their threats.

D. Your ministry

This includes all the work God has committed into your hands. It could be a role you are playing in your local church, or personal evangelism that God calls you to do for Him.

There are certain discouraging things the devil and the world will throw at you to try to make you stop your ministry. It could come in the form of blackmail, e.g. where secular grant makers threaten to withdraw funding if you don't denounce your biblical views on homosexuality. Or it could simply be gossip – malicious people spreading false rumours about you. You should not surrender to such intimidation; instead, you should release the situation into the hand of God and continue your good work.

Opposition may even come in the form of accusation and derision from fellow brethren. They may oppose your good work, but you should not stop. Fight for your ministry. In **Acts 4**, the disciples refused to be silenced by the council. They brought the situation to the church, who fought the threat of the enemy by prayer **(verses 24-31)**. Later, King Herod, who had been part of the conspiracy against Jesus **(Acts 4:27)**, died a horrible death **(Acts 12:23)**.

If you have the courage to stand up against all the attacks of the enemy confronting your ministry, you will see them no more.

E. Your salvation

You will need to fight for your salvation because the devil and the world want to turn you against God, to snatch your salvation from you. You will need to resist all the enemy throws at you to frustrate your salvation. To keep your salvation, you will need to stand firm in your faith.

Daniel 1:8 says: *"But Daniel purposed in his heart that he would not defile himself with the portion of the king's meat, nor with the wine which he drank: therefore he requested of the prince of the eunuchs that he might not defile himself."*

Daniel made up his mind not to corrupt himself with royal food and wine from the palace of the king. There were probably two reasons: the food might have included unclean meat forbidden by the Law of Moses, but the meat and wine would also have been ceremonially blessed in the name of the Babylonian idol, Bel. Daniel therefore chose to eat only vegetables, in order to keep himself from sin. He had to fight the temptation to eat the no-doubt delicious royal food, exercising self-control.

This needs a lot of internal strength. To remain in God's will, there are certain privileges you will need to turn down. You may need to refuse to accept what is yours by right, in order to be obedient to God. If you do so, God will rejoice over you.

Because Daniel made up his mind to please God, the flesh had no choice but to surrender to his will. If your will to please God is very strong, the flesh will have no choice but to cooperate with you. In Daniel 3, Daniel's three Hebrew friends refused to bow before an idol and so they were cast into the fire. But the fire of the enemy could not burn them, because the God they feared rules over fire. They fought the enemy by putting God before their

23

very lives. They fought their fear of fire and defeated it, remaining steadfast in their trust in God. God delivered them from the fire, but they were determined to obey God even if He didn't.

I pray that the grace of God will be so abundant upon your life that you will win all your battles, in Jesus' name.

F.   Your life's purpose

You were born into this world for a purpose, but you have to fight for your purpose on earth after you have discovered what it is. This is because the enemy wants to prevent you from fulfilling God's purpose for your life.

In **Genesis 37**, Joseph discovered the reason why he was born and then the enemy orchestrated a plan to frustrate it. His brothers sold him into slavery, but Joseph remained faithful to the Lord. When the devil discovered that he could not turn Joseph against God, he used Potiphar's wife to lure him into the sin of adultery, but the boy refused. He fought back. In Genesis 39, Joseph escaped the clutches of the wicked woman.

Joseph fought temptation and he won. You will need to continually fight the temptations the devil will throw in your way, as he tries to lure you into things that will abort your destiny.

G. Against curses

These are blessing blockers. There are spirits that sponsor curses. Once a curse is invoked, hell sends a spirit to start sponsoring its operation. The consequence of this is that the victim will discover that the blessings of God always elude him. Curses don't disappear on their own accord; the victim has to fight them.

Curses can be acquired or inherited. Acquired curses are those curses you have invited into your life through your own lifestyle. Inherited curses are those that pass into your life through the blood line of your parents. Accepting Jesus does not automatically set you free from a curse, but it equips you to break it and escape its dominion.

Some people have become born-again, yet their lives still manifest certain abnormalities in their family line. There is a need for the person to rise up and use the weapons of Jesus Christ to break such curses. In *1 Chronicles 4:9-12*, Jabez fought a curse his mother placed upon his destiny and he won. But until he rose up against it, the curse kept on operating and manipulating his destiny. You must rise up against curses; they don't disappear on their own. If you notice any abnormality in your life, you will need to rise up and fight it until your situation changes.

May God make you stronger than your enemy, in Jesus' name.

H. Against defeat

Defeat comes when the enemy succeeds in manipulating your victory. When you notice a defeat in any area of your life, you will need to fight it until you win. God does not expect you to accept defeat but to rise up against it.

In *Joshua 7*, Joshua lost a battle for the first time since he had started serving God. But instead of accepting the defeat, he rose up against it. He went to God to discover why he had been defeated. God made him aware of how Achan ensnared the whole nation of Israel through his sin of disobedience. If you have lost a battle, the reason may be that the enemy has subtly entered into certain areas of your life. When you notice a defeat in any of your struggles, consult God for the reason and mend your ways. After this – go for a rematch! Enter the battle again. Rise up to challenge your enemy.

For example, if you have searched for a job with no success, instead of crying and mourning over it, ask God to reveal the secret of your failure to you. When you find it, change your ways and apply for vacancies again. Victory is certain. You are not defeated until you accept the defeat. Your enemy is not a winner until you call him a winner.

I. For your business

Your business may come under the attack of the enemy, as he likes to undermine our faith by mining our bank balance! If your business stops making the profit that it used to, it might be that the enemy is at work.

Instead of closing it down, you will need to fight the spirit that is sponsoring its failure. In Luke 5, Peter worked all night but caught no fish. It was a business failure for him on that day. Suddenly, Jesus came to Peter to use his boat to speak to the people. Afterwards, He instructed Peter to spread his nets into the deep. Peter was reluctant, but still obeyed Jesus. Amazingly, the same nets that caught nothing now caught plenty of fish. The same lake that yielded no fish now gave up so many that Peter's net broke and the two boats nearly sank!

If you are convinced that God wants you to stay in the same business, decide to give it one last go. You will be amazed how the same business that yielded nothing in the past can change to make a profit. Refusal to quit positions you for a miracle. Situations that have not been cooperating with you will suddenly start cooperating, and the story will change.

May God make you laugh at your failures, in Jesus' name.

J. Against hardship

When the going gets tough, the tough get going. Do you know that saying? Well, you need to be ready to fight hardship and everything that makes your life difficult. When survival becomes hard, you must fight it and not give up. The devil orchestrates many kinds of suffering and has no mercy, so there is no wisdom in hoping it will go away of its own accord. The right thing to do is to rise against it and fight it until you defeat it.

2 Kings 4:1 says: *"Now there cried a certain woman of the wives of the sons of the prophets unto Elisha, saying, Thy servant my husband is dead; and thou knowest that thy servant did fear the LORD: and the creditor is come to take unto him my two sons to be bondmen."*

This woman faced suffering and shame. She had no money to feed her children or to settle the debt. But instead of giving up, she got up and went to a man of God to plead for help. She got her miracle. The woman refused to bow to pressure, and instead fought the ugly situation life threw at her. Her desperation for a solution led her to the right place where help was available.

If you can refuse to surrender, light will shine on your way and heaven will order your steps to where help is waiting for you. Arise and fight your lack, hardship, shame, fear and every manner of situation that threatens your life. You can win if you can stay in the fight. Fight those things that want to destroy your good testimony of what God has done for you. Arise and fight for your life. May God lead you to where help is available, in Jesus' name.

- 2 -

God Wants You to Win

> **Jeremiah 29:11**
> "For I know the thoughts that I think toward you, saith the LORD, thoughts of peace, and not of evil, to give you an expected end."

God wants to give you your expected end. God wants you to achieve what you aim at. He wants you to succeed. He wants you to win. Whatever you set out to achieve, God wants you to achieve it. He wants you to reach what you aim towards in life. He wants His purpose for your life to become a reality.

God has never lost a battle and He wants his children to also be perpetual winners. From eternity, God has a plan for how His children should always win. God is on your side. He wants you to beat the devil and all his schemes. God is fully aware that there are battles for you to fight in the journey of life, and He has made provision for your victory before you came into this world.

Exodus 15:3 says: *"The LORD is a man of war: the LORD is his name."*

The Lord is a fighter. He loves fighting battles for His children. God does not like His children to fight their battles on their own because they will not be able to win against stronger enemies. God wants His children to always win, so He wants to be the one fighting their battles. Jesus said, *"… without me ye can do nothing"* **(John 15:5)**.

2 Chronicles 20:15 says: *"And he said, Hearken ye, all Judah, and ye inhabitants of Jerusalem, and thou king Jehoshaphat, Thus saith the LORD unto you, Be not afraid nor dismayed by reason of this great multitude; for the battle is not yours, but God's."*

God fights the battles of His children for them. Whenever His children face a battle, He expects them to hand it over to Him. God wants to fight your battle for you so that you remain a winner.

In **Exodus 14:25** God's involvement on His children's side was so powerful that even Israel's enemy recognised that the Lord was fighting for them: *"… the Egyptians said, Let us flee from the face of Israel; for the LORD fighteth for them against the Egyptians."*

When God fights for you, your enemies will truly know that your God is a fighter.

In **Joshua 1:5** God promised Joshua that no man would be able to hinder him: *"There shall not any man be able to stand before thee all the days of thy life: as I was with Moses, so I will be with thee: I will not fail thee, nor forsake thee."*

Joshua never experienced defeat in his entire journey with God (except at the battle of Ai, which wasn't Joshua's fault). He was a perpetual winner. He defeated allied forces. He defeated every enemy that engaged him in battle because the Lord fought for him. The same promise remains valid in your life. God wants no man to hinder you in your entire journey on earth.

In order to make Jeremiah undefeatable, God strengthened him in a special way: *"For, behold, I have made thee this day a defenced city, and an iron pillar, and brasen walls against the whole land, against the kings of Judah, against the princes thereof, against the priests thereof, and against the people of the land"* **(Jeremiah 1:18)**.

God made Jeremiah like a walled city that can't easily be pulled down by the enemy. The same God has made you a fortified city that can't be destroyed by the enemy. If you can walk in the knowledge of what God has done in you, you will be undefeatable. You will never be afraid of battle in life. God wants you to win in life.

In **Deuteronomy 20:1**, God promised His people that they need not fear the strength of their enemies because He would fight for them: *"When thou goest out to battle against thine enemies, and seest horses, and chariots, and a people more than thou, be not afraid of them: for the LORD thy God is with thee, which brought thee up out of the land of Egypt."*

With God fighting for you, there is no battle too big and no enemy so great that you can't win. God will give you victory, irrespective of the nature or magnitude of the battle.

But you must be careful that the battle is one that God wants you to take on. **1 Samuel 30:8** says: *"And David enquired at the LORD, saying, Shall I pursue after this troop? Shall I overtake them? And he answered him, Pursue: for thou shalt surely overtake them, and without fail recover all."*

David consulted God before he fought the Amalekites. God told him to pursue them and that He would give David victory, and David would recover all the possessions and people that the Amalekites had captured.

No matter how long you have lost a blessing, God can help you to recover it. He can lead you to engage the thieves in battle and recover all that they have stolen from your life. Recovery is possible with God. Whatever battle that needs to be fought in order to recover all your losses is winnable for you, if you consult God first.

In **Joshua 7**, as we have read, Joshua lost a battle for the first time in his journey with God. When he asked God to show him the reason for his defeat, God told him what went wrong. There was a sin in the camp. God revealed the secret because He wanted Joshua to always win. So God told Joshua what to do in order to defeat his enemies. Joshua followed all the instructions from God and recorded a decisive victory.

God loves you just as much as Joshua – He has no favourites **(Romans 2:11)**. So He always wants you to win too. If you have lost a battle, you can talk to God and ask for the reason for your defeat, and you will be amazed how easy it will become for you to overcome the enemy. God does not want you to lose any battle against evil.

In **1 Samuel 1**, Hannah refused to surrender to infertility. She persisted in her prayer, and one day God arose for her. She recorded a decisive victory over barrenness. If you can refuse to accept defeat, God will lead you to the path of victory, at a time of His choosing. When it seems as if the enemy is having the upper hand in the battle, still refuse to accept defeat. Your faithfulness and persistency will provoke God to send you help: *"But thanks be to God, which giveth us the victory through our Lord Jesus Christ"* **(1 Corinthians 15:57)**.

God decided to settle your victory in all the battles of life once and for all, by sending Jesus to defeat the devil for ever. The devil is the author of all the battles and confrontations of life, whereas God is the author of peace *(1 Corinthians 14:33)*. But because Jesus has defeated the devil on the cross, you can now claim that victory against him whenever he wants to raise his head against you in battle. You are to stand on the victory Jesus has freely given you over the devil, and you will become undefeatable in all your battles.

John 16:33 says: *"These things I have spoken unto you, that in me ye might have peace. In the world ye shall have tribulation: but be of good cheer; I have overcome the world."*

Jesus told His disciples that He had accomplished what God sent him to do for us. He has overcome the world and the prince of this world, the devil. *Colossians 2:13-15* says: *"And you, being dead in your sins and the uncircumcision of your flesh, hath he quickened together with him, having forgiven you all trespasses; blotting out the handwriting of ordinances that was against us, which was contrary to us, and took it out of the way, nailing it to his cross; and having spoiled principalities and powers, he made a shew of them openly, triumphing over them in it."*

Jesus defeated the devil and all the hosts of hell so that you can operate in victory over them. When you face the devil in the name of Jesus, he flees from you *(James 4:7)*. With the knowledge of victory Jesus has given you, there is no battle you can't win in life.

What do you do to operate in the knowledge of the victory that Jesus has won for you against the devil? You are to start every battle against the devil from the victory side. That is, whenever you face any battle, start praising God and celebrate your victory over the devil. You don't need to struggle to fight the battle Jesus has already won for you; you only need to take advantage of the victory Jesus has given you.

The common mistake we make when we face Satan in the battle of life is that we think we have to fight him. We don't. We merely resist him – and God fights for us. If Satan discovers we are ignorant of the victory Jesus has given us over him, he starts presenting himself as a force to be reckoned with. But if he finds us confident in knowing the victory has already been won, he knows he has lost.

God wants you to win. He has given you the victory through Jesus. Your job is to take advantage of that victory.

May you remain undefeatable in life, in Jesus' name.

- 3 -

It is Possible

Luke 1:37

"For with God nothing shall be impossible."

You can win all your battles in life. It is possible to be a perpetual winner in life. It is possible for you to never record a defeat and to live in victory over all of life's challenges.

Philippians 4:13 says: *"I can do all things through Christ which strengtheneth me."*

We need to heed what the Bible says: "all things!" Not some things, but all, provided we don't fight in our own strength but that of Jesus.

In *Romans 8*, the Apostle Paul says: *"If God be for us, who can be against us? He that spared not his own Son, but delivered him up for us all, how shall he not with him also freely give us all things?… Nay, in all these things we are more than conquerors through him that loved us"* *(verses 31-37)*.

You can record success in all the trials of life. You can be healed of a sickness the doctors describe as incurable. You can defeat any opposition, no matter how big or powerful. Jesus who strengthens you can never run out of strength, so there is no battle that you will not have enough strength to win. No matter how strong your enemy is, you can defeat him!

GET THE MIND-SET OF A WINNER

You will need to develop the attitude of a winner. A champion athlete believes that he can always win the race, no matter how fast the other runners are. Your belief influences how you see your enemy and the situation around you.

In *1 Samuel*, Goliath challenged the nation of Israelites to a battle for supremacy. His intimidating utterances and appearance silenced the whole army of Israel. King Saul considered Goliath undefeatable – he saw him as a giant soldier with outstanding experience. But David had a different mind-set: *"David said to Saul, Let no man's heart fail because of him; thy servant will go and fight with this Philistine" (17:32)*.

Saul's reply revealed his defeatist mind-set: *"And Saul said to David, Thou art not able to go against this Philistine to fight with him: for thou art but a youth, and he a man of war from his youth" (17:33)*.

Saul saw David as no match for Goliath. But David had a different view of the whole situation – God's view. To David, the winner would be the one that almighty God supported. He knew the secret of victory in the battle of life. You must develop a mind-set that God will always fight for you, if you want to always win.

It is not a matter of who has longer experience, superior skill or greater strength, but who will God fight for. Have no consideration for defeat. Don't entertain the thought of possible defeat as you engage in the battles of life. Train your mind to think only of victory. God responds to faith. Jesus said: *"What things soever ye desire, when ye pray, believe that ye receive them, and ye shall have them"* **(Mark 11:24)**.

That is, do not entertain the possibility of rejection in your dealings with God. Develop a positive mind-set that God will do as you have asked Him to do. When you ask God for victory, don't consider the possibility of defeat. Develop a strong conviction that your desires have been granted by God and so they are achievable. Resist every arrow of evil imagination the enemy may want to throw at your mind. Refuse to believe his lies.

The only condition Jesus put on His promise of answered prayer in **Mark 11** is this: *"And when ye stand praying, forgive, if ye have ought against any: that your Father also which is in heaven may forgive you your trespasses. But if ye do not forgive, neither will your Father which is in heaven forgive your trespasses"* **(Mark 11:25-26)**.

Unforgiveness is the only barrier to God hearing your prayer, because if you do not forgive, then, the Father won't forgive you for your sins. Sin then becomes the blockage to your prayer being answered. So ensure you forgive, so that God can forgive you and hear your prayers.

Then, if Jesus is Lord of your life, you can know that God is on your side and will fight for you, because He does not break His promises.

BE BOLD

Now that you have set your mind on victory, be bold in your thoughts, words and actions. This will help you to resist any intimidation from the enemy when you engage him in battle. Speak boldly and walk boldly.

You can only be bold in the battle if you are confident of God's victory on your behalf. So boldness is an expression of faith in God, of your belief concerning the situation. When the enemy realises that you are not half-hearted or doubting, he will be convinced that you know what you are doing.

If you reply with boldness to people who challenge your faith, it convinces them that your faith is real. In **Acts 4:13**, when the people *"saw the boldness of Peter and John, and perceived that they were unlearned and ignorant men, they marvelled; and they took knowledge of them, that they had been with Jesus."*

Peter replied to his enemies with boldness, refusing to compromise his words about Jesus, showing no fear of the religious leaders despite the power they had. This impressed and amazed the religious leaders. If, like Peter, you show no fear of the opposition, they will instead fear you. The weapon of the Devil is fear, and when it fails, it puts his plans into disarray.

Similarly, boldness will turn you into an attacker instead of a defender. You will be the one firing the first shot in the battle, and this puts the enemy into a defensive position. In 1 Samuel 17:49 David was the first to attack and this caught Goliath off guard. Before Goliath could respond, David's stone had sunk into his head. The battle was over. Boldness quickens the battle.

BE COURAGEOUS

Joshua 1:6
"Be strong and of a good courage: for unto this people shalt thou divide for an inheritance the land, which I sware unto their fathers to give them."

Courage is the quality of mind or spirit that enables a person to face difficulty, danger, pain and any kind of challenging situation without fear. A man of courage is brave. Courage gives strength to fight despite the danger. It is not ignoring danger – it is refusing to give in to it. A courageous man is not put off when the odds are stacked against him. Courage is infectious. A courageous man will create courage in those around him, which is why every army needs a hero. Courage is another quality you need to always win in life.

How can you have courage? By realising, once again, that one with God is a majority – that God is with you: *"Have not I commanded thee? Be strong and of a good courage; be not afraid, neither be thou dismayed: for the Lord thy God is with thee whithersoever thou goest" **(Joshua 1:9)**.*

CREATE CONFIDENCE

Be a creator of confidence. This will encourage your supporters to carry on when the easiest thing to do is quit. When you create confidence, even the onlookers may join forces with you to help you fight your battle. A winner must be able to create confidence, for this motivates people to become your helpers.

When the Israelites were about to invade Canaan, they sent spies into the land to assess their enemies. But when the spies returned, they created fear in the minds of the Israelites because of their report about the strength of the Canaanites. But Caleb tried to create confidence in the people so that they would be motivated to join him in battle: *"Caleb stilled the people before Moses, and said, Let us go up at once, and possess it; for we are well able to overcome it" **(Numbers 13:30)**.*

He talked positively. He wanted the people to see that they were stronger than their enemies. On this occasion, the people refused to believe Caleb, and as a result, they had to live in the desert for another 40 years. But God pronounced a special blessing on Caleb, because of his faith *(Numbers 14:24)*.

A winner must be able to create confidence. He must be a faith booster.

The enemy will do all he can to prevent you from having enough confidence in yourself. He likes to use your weaknesses to deceive you into believing that you don't have what it takes to win in life. But don't listen to his lies! There is no limit to your potential with God. The only limitations are those you put on yourself by failing to believe what God can do.

There are treasures inside you – a store of good things that God can use to bring victory. But if you accept the deception of the devil, you will not manifest those treasures. Many people do not even attempt to fight for anything in life because they have been deceived into thinking that they don't have what it takes to win. Refuse to accept that you don't have the requirements for victory. Remove those things the devil is using to conceal your potential. God will not allow a battle that you can't win to come to you. God *"will not suffer you to be tempted above that ye are able; but will with the temptation also make a way to escape, that ye may be able to bear it" (1 Corinthians 10:13)*.

Get rid of self-pity. Get rid of a sense of inadequacy. Get rid of a sense of helplessness. If your sin is sapping your confidence, confess it and believe in God's forgiveness and cleansing *(1 John 1:9)*.

In **John 5:5-8**, a crippled man believed that he could not get healing because he had no one to help him. Jesus proved him wrong. In reality, it is God who you need to help you, not man. You are not helpless unless you believe so. The day you came to Jesus, helplessness disappeared in your life. The Lord became your helper **(Hebrews 13:6)**. There is no ingredient of victory you don't have. They are all inside of you, if you will let them out of yourself.

You have inside of you the strength to win, because the Holy Spirit lives within you. You are not what the devil says you are. You are loaded inside to defeat any devil. Leave all the excuses behind and start believing in the power of God's Spirit within you **(2 Corinthians 4:7)**.

BELIEVE THAT TOMORROW IS A NEW DAY

However long you have struggled with an issue, however long you have been defeated, tomorrow is a new day! *"The Lord's mercies... are new every morning"* **(Lamentations 3:22-24)**. How long the battle has been going on in your life does not matter. You can still win.

It is possible to come out of a problem of many years within hours. The fact that you have been suffering for ten years does not mean it will take the same ten years for you to come out of suffering. The problems of many years can disappear within a day.

Exodus 12:40 says the Israelites lived in bondage for 430 years, but it took God one night to free them. The disaster of many years ended with one act of God. You can come out of challenges of many years today, as you are reading this book. It is possible. If you are ready, God is also ready. The strength or length of the problem does not matter when God fights for you. You can see the end of your strong enemy now. You can have easy victory against a battle of many years, right now.

MIND YOUR WORDS

What you confess with your mind and mouth is vital to your victory. Through your words, you can make or unmake victory, because positivity builds faith and negativity destroys it. Don't allow the devil to put negative words into your mouth. Don't always say what you see with your eyes, because faith is a matter of being confident of what you cannot see *(Hebrews 11:1)*. A good situation may appear hopeless at the beginning, but as the situation matures the truth becomes visible. Your words can take you far away from victory. When situations become challenging, the devil will attempt to put wrong words inside your head and on your lips, but you must refuse to speak such words. Don't agree with the devil's deception.

CHOOSE WISELY

Choose to accept faith in all situations. Faith is far better than unbelief. Trust is better than doubt. Hope is better than hopelessness. Unbelief breeds fear and anxiety. It causes sleepless nights and in time, it could lead to worry and depression. When a situation presents you with a choice between faith and unbelief, choose faith. Choose to believe that you will succeed, even when you don't know how it will come to pass. Choose to believe that you will not be defeated, even though you have no idea how to win. It gives strength to your heart and helps you retain control of your emotions. Fight to keep control of your emotions in all situations, and you will remain governable by the Holy Spirit, rather than being ruled by your emotions.

ACCEPT GOD'S SOVEREIGNTY

God is sovereign and He can do as He pleases in the affairs of men. God can overrule your unbelief to send you help for victory. It is true that your faith matters, but you can still win even when your faith level goes down. Why? Because of God's compassion, and His promise to be faithful to those who love Him, even when we're unfaithful to Him *(2 Timothy 2:13)*.

In *Genesis 18:10-14*, despite the fact that Sarah laughed and could not believe that God could give her a child in old age, she still received her miracle. God is in charge. He overrules our mistakes and failures to fulfil His own plans. Don't let the devil convince you that you can't win because your faith is low. You can still win in life, even when your faith is not very strong. Cry to God for God mercy, instead of accepting that your faith can't handle certain situations. God is a God of both the strong and the weak.

TRUST IN GOD'S IMPARTIALITY

Joshua 1:5
"There shall not any man be able to stand before thee all the days of thy life: as I was with Moses, so I will be with thee: I will not fail thee, nor forsake thee."

As God gave victory to Moses, so he gave victory to Joshua. God has enabled many people to win in life and He can do the same for you. Place your confidence in this. The reason why God has let you know what He did in the lives of those who came before you is to assure you that He wants to do the same in your life.

Some of the greatest heroes of the Bible were weak and sinful people, yet God transformed them into winners. If God did that for them, then He will do the same for you.

Just as God ensured that Jabez defeated a curse placed on him by his mother *(1 Chronicles 4:10)*, so He will enable you to break all the curses that are hindering your life. Through God's help, Job triumphed over satanic attack *(Job 42)* despite all he suffered, and the same God will help you to defeat every satanic attack in any area of your life. He is a good God to everybody, not just to somebody.

Through the intervention of God, the Red Sea parted *(Exodus 14)*. The same God will make a way through everything in your life that is standing as a barrier to victory, like God made a way through the Red Sea. Just as God saved His people from the Egyptian army, so He can save you from whatever peril you are in. As we saw in 1 Samuel 1, God gave Hannah victory over her barrenness. She won the battle to have a child. The same God that did it for Hannah is ready to do it for you. Trust Him and you will see yourself celebrating victory over a barren life.

Ever since Satan began his work in the world, the Lord has been defeating his schemes across the globe. The Lord has destroyed the work of Satan in any form it has appeared in the lives of God's people. The same God will destroy every work of the enemy in any area of your life. Just trust Him.

- 4 -

Enforcement

John 8:44

"Ye are of your father the devil, and the lusts of your father ye will do. He was a murderer from the beginning, and abode not in the truth, because there is no truth in him. When he speaketh a lie, he speaketh of his own: for he is a liar, and the father of it."

This verse states that the devil, your real enemy, never works in the truth. What is the truth? Jesus is the truth. What God says concerning you is the truth. So the truth is that God has given you victory through Jesus Christ. It is the truth that you are more than a conqueror. It is true that you are a victor. It is true that you are a son of God, a child of God, a brother or sister of Christ, a co-heir with Christ, a partaker of the inheritance of the saints.

But the devil never works in the truth, though he knows the truth. Sickness knows that you are healed by the wounds of Jesus, but it still may attack you. Poverty knows that through the poverty of Jesus you have been made rich, but it will still attempt to rule your life. It is the truth that Jesus has overcome the world for you, yet the world will do all it can to overcome you.

You will need to acquire what Jesus has acquired for you by enforcing it. Enforcement becomes necessary when the guilty party refuses to accept the judgement of the judge. Two thousand years ago, Jesus judged sickness, poverty, lack, fear, death and all the works of the devil. Jesus did this through His life on the earth, His death on the cross and His resurrection from the grave. But because all the evil of this world will not recognise the judgement passed against them concerning you, you will need to enforce the judgement passed by Jesus against them. Unless you enforce your *"inheritance of the saints"* **(Colossians 1:12)**, God's enemies will attempt to operate in certain areas of your life. It is time to rise against the devil and all his cohorts, because God *"hath delivered us from the power of darkness, and hath translated us into the kingdom of his dear Son"* **(Colossians 1:13)**.

NO NEGOTIATION

Galatians 5:1
"Stand fast therefore in the liberty wherewith Christ hath made us free, and be not entangled again with the yoke of bondage."

Jesus has given you liberty from every aspect of the work of the devil, and you must stand on this. Don't negotiate for what you have already been given. Refuse to negotiate for your healing. You have been healed since the days Jesus was on earth over two thousand years ago. Stand on this.

Reject every contrary opinion to what Jesus has done for you. You will be negotiating away your healing and blessings if you open yourself up to the possibility that what men are saying could be the truth, despite it being contrary to what Jesus has done for you. Don't accept or walk in any opinions that contradict God's truth, no matter how reasonable they may sound. Don't negotiate with poverty. Don't negotiate with failure. Take your stand on what you believe. You will be negotiating away your victory if you accept that you cannot win. The truth is that you have been declared a winner by Jesus even before you were born. Stand on the truth.

NO RETREAT, NO SURRENDER

Mark 5:25-29
"And a certain woman, which had an issue of blood twelve years, and had suffered many things of many physicians, and had spent all that she had, and was nothing bettered, but rather grew worse, when she had heard of Jesus, came in the press behind, and touched his garment. For she said, If I may touch but his clothes, I shall be whole. And straightway the fountain of her blood was dried up; and she felt in her body that she was healed of that plague."

Unless your problem disappears from your life, never stop seeking a solution. Despite a series of failed attempts to get healed, the woman with the blood haemorrhage kept on looking for a solution. She never stopped until she got her healing. When you start fighting the work of Satan in your life, don't stop until you record the victory.

EXALT THE JUDGEMENT

Revelation 12:11
"And they overcame him by the blood of the Lamb, and by the word of their testimony; and they loved not their lives unto the death."

47

The Word of God is the judgement. What the Word of God says concerning your situation is the judgement. Whatever happens in the battle, always raise the judgement. Always declare what the judgement of God says concerning the situation. Let the Word of God become louder than the words of the world. Respect what the Word of God says concerning the situation. Disrespect and disregard the words of men that contradict God's Word.

Saul's failing was to listen to men instead of God: *"And Saul said unto Samuel, I have sinned: for I have transgressed the commandment of the Lord, and thy words: because I feared the people, and obeyed their voice"* **(1 Samuel 15:24)**.

Continually repeating what God says about a situation soon destroys the power behind it. Send the Word of God into that storm and the power sponsoring it will flee. Exalt the Word of God above that of men, because God's Word is powerful: *"For the word of God is quick, and powerful, and sharper than any two-edged sword, piercing even to the dividing asunder of soul and spirit, and of the joints and marrow, and is a discerner of the thoughts and intents of the heart"* **(Hebrews 14:12)**.

God's Word always accomplishes God's purpose for it: *"So shall my word be that goeth forth out of my mouth: it shall not return unto me void, but it shall accomplish that which I please, and it shall prosper in the thing whereto I sent it"* **(Isaiah 55:11)**.

Face the enemy with the Word, as Jesus did in **Luke 4:4**: *"It is written…"* Tell the situation what is written concerning it in the Word of God, *"For the word of the Lord is right; and all his works are done in truth"* **(Psalm 33:4)**.

SPEAK AS GOD'S REPRESENTATIVE

Psalms 82:6
"I have said, Ye are gods; and all of you are children of the most High."

You are a 'god' because you are a representative of God, an ambassador of Christ **(2 Corinthians 5:20)**. You are to speak as God would speak to a situation. How does God speak to a situation?

In **Genesis 1:2-3** God spoke creation into being: *"And the earth was without form, and void; and darkness was upon the face of the deep. And the Spirit of God moved upon the face of the waters. And God said, Let there be light: and there was light."*

From emptiness, God spoke light into existence. God spoke with the mind of creation. Through His Word, He creates light. You also should speak with the mind of creation into your emptiness. When you face a situation that is devoid of good things that you desire, speak with the mind of creation. Speak with hope to a hopeless situation. Speak with the mind of fruitfulness to your barren land. Many great things of this world started from emptiness. With your word you can create what you desire, if your heart is in line with God's heart for a situation. As you ignore what the situation looks like and begin speaking your desire, soon things will begin to fall into place for your sake.

God speaks authoritatively. He speaks with commanding tone. You must speak with authority to the situation. Speak without giving attention to what the situation says. Don't let the situation intimidate you.

BE FOCUSED

Light can generate more power when all its rays are directed towards one point. When you direct all your attention towards a situation, soon, victory will come. You must control and focus your thoughts, emotions and actions towards your challenges. Don't let the devil distract you from your course. Be focused. You can make a big impact if you are able to focus every fibre inside of you towards a point. The devil can't withstand an undivided heart, and that is why he wants you to be distracted and diverted. **Psalm 86:11** says: *"Teach me thy way, O Lord; I will walk in thy truth: unite my heart to fear thy name."*

The source of distraction is doing many things at the same time. Don't get too busy with so many things. Avoid situations that will divide your attention onto many issues. Avoid thinking one thing and doing another. Fight with the whole of your being.

ALTER YOUR VIEW

Romans 4:17
"As it is written, I have made thee a father of many nations, before him whom he believed, even God, who quickeneth the dead, and calleth those things which be not as though they were."

You need to see the situation in the light of your expectation. Start treating the situation as if you have already accomplished your goal, because *"with God, nothing shall be impossible"* **(Luke 1:37)**. Begin to walk in your victory. Call things which are not as though they were. If it is sickness you are fighting, start seeing your sick body as already healed. If it is joblessness you are fighting, start seeing yourself as a man with a good job. If it is a shrinking business, see a growing business. If your marriage is troubled, begin to see it as healing.

Start addressing yourself in the light of your expectation. Express your certainty of victory and see your impossible situation as possible. Gradually, you are preparing the situation around you for the miracles that will soon be born into your life. Call the situation the name you want, not the one the enemy dictates. Refuse to agree with the enemy that your matter is hopeless. Don't say I am weak, but I am strong.

BY FAITH NOT BY SIGHT

2 Corinthians 5:7
"For we walk by faith, not by sight."

This verse indicates that you should walk by what you believe, not by what you see. If you believe that you are healed, as stated in the Word of God, then walk by that and ignore the fact that you still feel sick. If you believe the report of God concerning your situation, walk by it and ignore the contrary report of the enemy.

As you maintain the pressure on the enemy through trusting God, you are winning, though, it may not manifest immediately. You might not have reached where you want to be, but you are no longer where you used to be. Things are changing for you. You are making progress. By normal sight, the situation may appear the same, but by faith, there is a lot of change going on. Don't agree with the picture the enemy is showing you as the battle rages on. Keep on fighting and soon, you will notice the positive changes.

IGNORE APPEARANCES

1 Samuel 17:4-6
"And there went out a champion out of the camp of the Philistines, named Goliath, of Gath, whose height was six cubits and a span. And he had an helmet of brass upon his head, and he was armed with a coat of mail; and the weight of the coat was five thousand shekels of brass. And he had greaves of brass upon his legs, and a target of brass between his shoulders."

Goliath dressed in an intimidating manner. His battle armour was intended to intimidate David and instil fear in him. Unfortunately for him, despite his appearance of strength, it only took one stone from David to bring him down.

The problems of life come in different disguises. Challenges come in many forms. For example, a sickness may come with clothing that could be described as incurable and terminal. Poverty may appear in somebody's life with a dress that could be described as terrible. All the adjectives used to describe a situation refer to the way it appears to the victim. Whether it is called critical, terrible or impossible, it may need only one blow from you in order to fall.

Jesus has healed you of every manner of illness, irrespective of how it might be described. Jesus has given you victory over all the battles of life, irrespective of the size of the battle. Exercise your dominion over the situation and it will bow. Ignore the seriousness of the situation and enforce the judgement of God concerning it, as it is written in His Word.

BREAK THE RESISTANCE

Continual application of effort breaks down resistance. There is a power sponsoring every bad event of life. There is a power behind your challenges. When the power fails to surrender easily, you will need to apply greater force to break the resistance.

When situations do not change as you desire, it may be time to apply the decree. **Job 22:28** says: *"Thou shalt also decree a thing, and it shall be established unto thee: and the light shall shine upon thy ways."*

Through the decree, you will speedily force the situation to conform to your expectation. Start issuing your decree. Command the situation as you wish. Through decree, you will be able to decide with authority how you want the situation to progress. You make your decree by standing on the Word of God. Through decree, you will order the situation to follow a certain direction. Decree that you will never be sick again. Decree that all forces sponsoring your problem should enter into everlasting captivity. Decree a termination to every evil process initiated from hell to make your life miserable. Decree that you will always be on top, as it is written in the Word of God, decree confusion into your enemy's camp. Command the plant God has not planted in your life to be rooted out. Establish your expectation through decree.

IT IS A WAR

Matthew 11:12
"And from the days of John the Baptist until now the kingdom of heaven suffereth violence, and the violent take it by force."

War involves confrontation, hostility and aggression. A lot of struggles are involved in fighting a war. Spiritual violence is needed to record victory over the forces of 'aliens'. By aliens, I mean the things that are foreign to the life of a victorious Christians – things that should be alienated from your life. These include sicknesses, lack and every manner of work of Satan. You must be aggressive and passionate in contending with the situation you are opposing. You must show to that problem that you hate it with a passion. You must carry on a prolonged and sustained attack on your situation, until you get the right result.

You must arm yourself with knowledge of the judgement of God against your challenges. You must not allow breathing space for your enemy. Fight very hard against those challenges that trouble your mind. Fight your enemy with your mouth and mind until something you desire happens. Fight repeatedly until you put an end to that evil in your life.

- 5 -

The Attitude that Wins

An attitude is a settled way of thinking or feeling that reflects in your behaviour. It is your repeated way of doing things. Your views and actions are dictated by your attitude, and your chances of winning in life are determined by your attitude.

There are two types of attitude: positive and negative. When you ask a man to describe how he sees a cup that is half full of water, his response will reveal the kind of attitude he has. If he has a positive attitude towards life, he will describe the glass as half full of water. That is positive. But if he has a negative attitude towards life, he will describe the glass as half empty of water. While the two answers are valid descriptions of the same object, each answer also indicates a different attitude and different view of the water inside the glass.

A man of positive attitude will always view the situation from a positive perspective, while the man of negative attitude will view it in a negative way. If you are going to win in life, you need to ensure that you operate your life with a positive attitude. The impact of attitude on your life can't be overemphasized.

A negative attitude can turn a simple problem into a complicated one. It hinders free flowing of good ideas. On the other hand, a positive attitude can turn a problem into an opportunity. A positive attitude can create abundance out of nothing. A negative attitude can turn a solution into a problem, and bring pollution into clean water. The right attitude can turn an enemy into a friend. People withdraw from a man of negative attitude, because he wears down their spirit and dissipates their determination. Your attitude will determine what you attract. A positive attitude attracts the positive things of life, things that will benefit your life. A negative attitude attracts negative things of life – things that will rob you of your destiny.

A winning attitude has the following characteristics:

1. POSITIVE BELIEF

We need a belief in victory and not defeat. A victorious man believes that he will succeed in whatever he lays his hands on, though; he may not understand how it will be accomplished. He sees himself as undefeatable in life. He also believes in what God says concerning his life. He believes that he is the head and not the tail. He believes that Jesus has made him rich and so, he can never be poor. He believes in riches and not poverty. He believes in health and not sickness. He truly believes that he has been healed by the stripes (wounds) of Jesus. This attitude will affect your state of mind. It will make you develop a positive mind towards whatever you do in life. Soon, what you believe will be attracted towards your life.

2. POSITIVE AFFIRMATION

This is a declaration that something is true and exists. The attitude that wins affirms that it is true that God has made us winners, and that the victory is real. We need to work in the reality of victory.

Even when situations become ugly, stick to this affirmation. A winner will continually declare what God says and not what the situations say.

3. RADIATES ENTHUSIASM

Enthusiasm is the great excitement for or interest in a subject or cause. Someone with an attitude that wins is always enthusiastic. He has great interest in whatever he does. He is lively and active. He enjoys what he is doing. This will make him alert. Such people rarely miss opportunities. To win in life, you must be fervent and passionate about your cause.

4. A SENSE OF HUMOUR

This is not about cracking jokes but about maintaining your joy in the midst of turmoil. Someone with a winning attitude always laughs. He laughs in the face of what looks like defeat. He laughs at the devil, he laughs at his enemies, he laughs at his battle, and he laughs at things the world throws at him to make him sad. Sometimes, he laughs at himself, especially when he gets things wrong. He resorts to laughter instead of becoming bitter. He has the ability to cause amusement. He is always in a good mood. He is full of smiles. People always want to have him around them. This attitude draws helpers and creates an atmosphere around you that's conducive to success. You will always see situations working out for you.

5. TAKES RESPONSIBILITY

Someone with a winning attitude never blames anybody for his predicament. He takes responsibility for his mistakes. When he gets things wrong, he focuses on himself, not an outsider.

This helps him to become better. He takes responsibility for all his actions and he wants to find out how to improve. He will always come out greater and wiser whenever he messes things up. There are people that, in their own view, have never done anything wrong. They always blame other people and never blame themselves. This is not an attitude of winners. Winners learn from their mistakes and become better. They will soon turn failure into victory.

6. IS A CHASER

An attitude that wins always chases a plan and never waits for it. A chaser pursues. He hunts after his dream. Treasures of life are located in hidden places and only those that hunt them will discover them. Unless you chase a thief, you may never catch him to recover your stolen blessings. Trust God to order your steps and arise to chase your dream. You will need to chase healing in order to come out of sickness. You will need to chase a career or business in order to come out of poverty.

7. HAS A SOLUTION FOCUS

An attitude that wins focuses on solutions and not problems. Some people are good at analysing problems but they have no idea on how to come up with a solution. The world has got enough problems; what it is looking for is the way to overcome those problems. Instead of magnifying the problem, spend your energy on seeking the solution. It may be true that there is a problem, and it is good to understand exactly what the problem is before choosing the right solution, but the wise question is: what can we do to solve it? Focus on solutions instead of being overwhelmed by the problem.

8. HOPES

An attitude that wins is full of hope. Hopeful people are always optimistic. They are people of possibility. They have an expectation that situations will turn out in their favour. A man of hope always looks forward for good news. He will never get carried away by the prevailing situation. Hope helps you foresee victory. It makes you act in victory even when there is no sign of it. Hope gives strength to your bones and makes you able to resist the enemy's attack on your mind. A man of winning attitude has hope and he has the best reason for being hopeful – his hope is in the Lord. This makes it impossible for anybody to defeat his hope. Life without hope can never win.

9. EXPLORES

Someone with an attitude that wins explores all possibilities when situations become critical. When his method fails to work, he explores the possibility of another method. He will not conclude that there is no other way forward. When a mountainous problem refuses to shift position, it may be an indication to you that your method is not working and that there is a need to explore other possibilities, other methods. This attitude opens the door to creativity. When you accept that there should be another way, then you open up your spirit for creative ideas.

10. IS TEACHABLE

An attitude that wins learns from other people, absorbing new ideas. Such people are teachable because they accept that they don't know all the answers, so they need to seek those who do have the answer. Most, if not all of what you are struggling to achieve has already been accomplished by somebody else, somewhere else. If you can be teachable, you will learn from those who have gone ahead of you in life, and you will be able to escape the frustration they experienced when they were in your position.

11. HAS GOOD SELF-ESTEEM

Your self-esteem is about your attitude towards yourself. It describes how you see yourself. It is a self-evaluation. The person with an attitude that wins has good self-esteem. That is, the person has a good evaluation of himself or herself. Such people consider themselves worthy, of value, because God values them. They see their personal capacity. They have confidence in their ability to succeed in life.

A person with good self-esteem says: "I am able, I am ready for success, I am attractive, I am better than my competitors, I have all that is needed to win in life, I am a child of God, I can do all things through Christ who strengthens me," etc.

You will need a good self-esteem if you are going to always win. This is because the enemy is intimidating in his approach. The devil always looks down on those who want to rise against his kingdom, and wants you to think that you are not worthy to win. When the world says you haven't got what it takes to win, it is the way you see yourself that will carry you forward. The way you see yourself is more important than the way the world sees you. Build your self-esteem by looking at yourself the way God looks at you – read all His Word says about His sons and daughters. Tell yourself that you are anointed by God, so you have all that is needed to win in life.

12. IS FRIENDLY

An attitude that wins is friendly and able to accommodate people. A friendly person is able to tolerate others. He can easily journey with people. To succeed in life you will need helpers, and for them to stay with you will require a conducive and friendly atmosphere. Avoid being hostile to people, otherwise no one will come to help you.

13. BOUNCES BACK

This is the ability to recover quickly from shock and any form of disappointment. A winning attitude is one that is able to overcome setbacks. It does not stay too long at the junction of frustration. Resilient people are able to quickly regain their lost courage and confidence. When they make negative confessions, they will speedily get themselves back into a positive frame of mind and change their confession. To win will require the ability to quickly recover lost hope. When you are down due to incessant frustration and attacks from the enemy, you need to quickly restore your confidence, recover your determination and move on with life. People that win don't stay frustrated and confused. They bounce back quickly.

14. PUTS IN THE BEST

An attitude that wins gives its best at all times. Your best may not be enough, but always put your best into whatever you do. Fight the enemy to the best of your ability – don't be half-hearted. Use your best resources in the battle of life. Put in your best energy, time, money and any other resources that can aid your success. Launch out fully against your enemy. Don't have any reservations. It is only your best that guarantees victory in the battle of life.

15. KEEPS A POSITIVE, CALM APPROACH

Your attitude determines how you will approach a situation. Your approach determines your method and the way you will handle issues. An attitude that wins must always approach a situation calmly. You must calm down and be gentle in approach. This positions you to access hidden things in the situation. Avoid rushing through an issue. It will only lead to disorder and you may miss important things. When you don't know all the details, be open to any possibility. Avoid making rash conclusions before you have assessed the situation properly. Be positive and apply positive methods. Have the mind of possibility in all situations.

- 6 -

The Power of the Will

Willpower is your inner strength and determination that enables you to pursue your wishes or plans until you succeed. It is a very strong resolve to do something.

Willpower enables you to make decisions and carry them out. It gives you the power to take action and perform tasks and plans, despite inner resistance, discomfort, laziness or difficulties. It is the mental muscle that makes people stubbornly carry on in the face of hindrances and opposition. You can't always win in life if your willpower is weak. The bigger the task, the more willpower is necessary. You will need strong willpower to refuse to bow to powerful opponents.

Let's look at the differences between weak willpower and strong willpower...

A. WEAK WILLPOWER

Your willpower is weak if you manifest the following in the pursuit of your purpose:

1. Procrastination

This is when you delay an action or certain responsibilities. People that procrastinate always say: "I will do it next time."

2. Excuses

These are the reasons given to justify inaction and lack of responsibility. You can always find good reasons for not doing the right things at the right time.

3. Lack of focus

A person of weak willpower moves from plan to plan without getting anywhere. Every little challenge makes him abandon the plan and develop another one. It is only a matter of time before he will abandon the new plan and seek another one. Such people move round the circle of life with no success.

4. Laziness

A man of weak willpower will manifest laziness. He will be idle when he is supposed to work on the plan. Even when he works on the plan, he will be too slow.

5. Distraction

A man of weak willpower is easily distracted. His mind is not fully committed to the cause. Every little challenge distracts him. He easily loses the track of events. Soon, he will mess up the whole plan.

6. Double-mindedness

A man of weak willpower has divided loyalties and unresolved priorities. He has so many alternative plans. He does not fully believe that things will work out well for him. He is never sure of his purpose. He is undecided. He staggers in the face of every little challenge.

7. Easily giving up

A man of weak willpower gives up his plan whenever situations go wrong. He lacks courage and self-motivation.

8. Incompleteness

A man of weak willpower never completes a task. He has a history of many abandoned projects. When he chases a vision, he will do it to a certain stage, and then moves to another before finishing the first one.

9. Lack of passion

A man of weak willpower has no passion for his cause. He is always reluctant. He is not aggressive and always very cold. He lacks inner drive.

10. Negative attitude

A man of weak willpower usually has a gloomy, pessimistic attitude. He will always find a justification for every bad thing he does, and expects that he will never achieve what he sets out to achieve. But he never takes responsibility for his failure. He will always put the blame on another person whenever situations go wrong.

B. STRONG WILLPOWER

The attributes of strong willpower include the following:

1. Self-control

A man of strong willpower demonstrates self-control in situations of temptation, stress or danger. He is able to put himself under the guidance and dictates of the Holy Spirit. He is not ready to mess up his plan.

> *1 Corinthians 9:27*
> *"But I keep under my body, and bring it into subjection: lest that by any means, when I have preached to others, I myself should be a castaway."*

It takes self-control to prevent your body from dictating how you should handle situations. To win in life, you will need to deny your body control over your life. Strong willpower will enable you to frustrate every attempt of your body to deflect you from the path you have chosen.

2. Consistency

The ability to stick to your values. Such a man does not contradict himself. He is able to maintain focus and continually apply effort until he succeeds. It needs strong willpower not to shift your position, even though there may be strong pressure to do so.

> *Job 1:22*
> *"In all this Job sinned not, nor charged God foolishly."*

Job was consistent in his testimony. He never wavered in his comments about God. For you to maintain your comments, opinions and reactions in the face of changing events will require strong willpower.

3. Endurance

This is the ability to bear pain, hardship or adversity. Strong willpower helps you to endure every challenge on the way.

> ### James 1:12
> "Blessed is the man that endureth temptation: for when he is tried, he shall receive the crown of life, which the Lord hath promised to them that love him."

Endurance will bring success. It enables you to resist every temptation to quit.

4. Immovability

This is the ability to hold fast, to 'stick to your guns', to keep to your decisions. It needs strong willpower to not let go of your plan, whatever the opposition.

> ### 1 Thessalonians 5:21
> "Prove all things; hold fast that which is good."

To win always will require your ability to hold onto your course, not letting go.

5. Perseverance

This is the ability to continually apply effort. Similar to endurance, it means withstanding the discouragements and every kind of difficulty. Perseverance will enable you to keep going to the end. It will help you to always complete a task with success. It will wear out your opponents.

> ### Ephesians 6:18
> "Praying always with all prayer and supplication in the Spirit, and watching thereunto with all perseverance and supplication for all saints…"

To watch with all perseverance implies not surrendering or falling for the temptation to quit. It needs a strong will.

6. Self-motivation

This is the ability to move yourself forward towards a goal. When there is no one else to motivate you or encourage you, then you will need to push yourself forward.

> ### 1 Samuel 30:6
> *"And David was greatly distressed; for the people spake of stoning him, because the soul of all the people was grieved, every man for his sons and for his daughters: but David encouraged himself in the LORD his God."*

Everybody around David became negative, so David encouraged himself and made himself seek God for solution. A strong will helps you to carry on when there is no one to support or encourage you. In the absence of any external force to move you forward, you have to rely on your inner strength. You push yourself to work towards a goal and to act rightly.

7. Patience

This is the ability to be calm under pressure. A patient man does not complain because he is able to tolerate adverse situations. He is able to cope with delays and provocation. He would rather be patient than fail in his purpose. He believes it is only a matter of time before his difficulties will come to an end.

> ### Hebrews 6:15
> *"And so, after he had patiently endured, he obtained the promise."*

Patience is a product of strong willpower.

8. Commitment

This is the act of binding yourself to a course of action or a purpose. It requires sincere and steadfast effort towards a cause. It makes you invest all your resources in a cause. It will require a strong will to manifest commitment towards a purpose.

> ### Luke 18:28-31
> "Then Peter said, Lo, we have left all, and followed thee. And he said unto them, Verily I say unto you, There is no man that hath left house, or parents, or brethren, or wife, or children, for the kingdom of God's sake, Who shall not receive manifold more in this present time, and in the world to come life everlasting. Then he took unto him the twelve, and said unto them, Behold, we go up to Jerusalem, and all things that are written by the prophets concerning the Son of man shall be accomplished."

Due to their commitments, the disciples had to leave all they had to follow Jesus. It requires a strong will to pay such a huge price. Jesus told them that there will always be sweet rewards for genuine commitment. To win always will require a certain price and only strong willpower will make you ready for such commitment.

9. Refusal to give in

This is the ability to try again and again and again, to never give up when situations become unfavourable. If you are forced to retreat, you will come back again due to strong willpower.

> ### Micah 7:8
> *"Rejoice not against me, O mine enemy: when I fall, I shall arise; when I sit in darkness, the LORD shall be a light unto me."*

To rise again will require strong willpower and determination never to quit.

10. Resolution

This is the ability to be firm, unmovable and determined in pursuit of your goal. Quitting or giving up is not an option for a resolute man. His mind is made up. He is decisive and stubborn, undeterred by any form of opposition.

In **2 Kings 2:1-6**, Elijah discouraged Elisha from following him three times, but Elisha refused to yield. Elisha was resolute about getting a double portion of anointing from Elijah. His willpower was very strong. He got what he was aiming for at last. He won.

DEVELOPING STRONG WILLPOWER

Strong willpower is needed if you want to win in life. Without it, every little challenge will set you back or knock you off track. Without strong willpower, you will not be able to press on until you win. To develop strong willpower:

1. Get your priorities right

Know why you want to do what you want to do. You will have to major on the major issues and minor on the minor issues. Avoid chasing first what should come last.

2. Develop a mind-set of optimism

Be a person of hope. Always expect a favourable outcome in all that you do. Whatever the situation, assure yourself of a positive result.

> ### Romans 8:28
> "And we know that all things work together for good to them that love God, to them who are the called according to his purpose."

3. Decide to be the best in all you do

Avoid mediocrity. Put your best effort into everything you do and use your best resources in every task.

4. Rule your emotions

Emotions determine your reaction to a situation. Always be calm in all circumstances. Don't let your emotions override your ability to make rational decisions. Be still, and avoid allowing the situation to dictate your reaction. Remember that things are not always as they appear. Do not allow yourself to exaggerate the problems.

5. Never accept defeat

Even when it seems you have been defeated, seek the opportunity for a re-match. Whenever you lose a case, look for the possibility of an appeal. When a situation turns out negatively for you, always ask yourself what you can do differently and better next time.

6. Live for the day

Let the past be the past. Don't accept that because you have failed before that you will always fail. Treat every new opportunity as new. Avoid carrying yesterday's failures into the future.

7. Be a success-orientated person

The driving force of such a person is to achieve success. He will not let any opposition get in his way. He explores all the possibilities for being successful in all he does. He is only interested in how to have success and whatever is contrary to that is not welcome.

8. Renew your mind

Get rid of all negativities that get in the way of success. Replace negative thoughts with positive ones. Examples of such negative thoughts that you must replace with positive thoughts include:

Negative thoughts	Positive thoughts
a. I can't	I can
b. I am unable	I am able
c. People hate me	People love me
d. Things are bad	Things are good
e. People are terrible	People are good
f. I am defeated	I am a victor
g. There is no way out	There is a way out
h. My plan will not work	My plan will work
i. Nobody can solve it	Someone can solve it
j. Supposing I fail	Supposing I succeed
k. I don't have enough resources	I have enough resources
l. I can't do all things	I can do all things
m. Things are getting worse	Things are getting better
n. This life is difficult	This life is easy

It should be noted that developing a positive mind-set is not the same as operating in self-deception. You need to accept the reality of a situation, but train yourself to approach it from the side of success.

As a man thinks, so he is. If you fill your mind with thoughts of failure, your life will attract failures. You can decide to walk in human wisdom or in the truth of the Word of God. A positive mind-set will enable you to walk in the light of the Word of God, not according to the dictates of life's difficulties. Don't allow a life situation to dictate how you handle it – instead, believe what God says about it.

> ### 2 Kings 4:26
> *"Run now, I pray thee, to meet her, and say unto her, Is it well with thee? Is it well with thy husband? Is it well with the child? And she answered, It is well..."*

This section of **2 Kings** is about a Shunammite woman who has just lost her son. The man of God sent his servant to ask her if everything was all right and the woman answered: "It is well." To say that it is well when your child has died sounds unrealistic, but it revealed the kind of mind-set the woman had. She had trained her mind to be positive even in a negative situation, to keep her faith in God.

At the end of the story, God honoured her faith; He used Elisha to bring the child back to life. A positive mind-set can turn situations around.

9. Overhaul your belief system

Everyone lives according to his or her beliefs. What you believe will determine your attitude and the way you handle situations. If you want to always win in life, you must adjust your belief system.

Examples of things you must believe include: possibility, not impossibility; love, not hate; good, not evil; strength, not weakness; health, not sickness; progress, not stagnancy; advancement, not backwardness; success; not failure; prosperity, not poverty; friendship, not enmity.

Similarly, believe that God wants you to win in life and that He wants you to live a life of the best. Believe in what the Word of God says about situations in your life. The Word of God calls you a victor. Believe it and walk in it.

10. Right focus

This is about attention. Avoid giving attention to what will not promote your victory. There are things that build and there are things that destroy. There are people who promote vision and people who destroy vision. There are things that work for you and things that work against you. Invest your attention in things and people that will promote your victory.

Don't give your attention to things and people that are working against your life. Focus on things that build and not things that destroy. Invest in those things that motivate you and not things that demotivate. Encourage yourself based on those things that promote your vision, and don't get discouraged by the things that oppose you. Don't spend your precious time on people who hate you when there are many people that really love you. Get your focus right.

THE TEST OF WILLPOWER

To always win, you must be able to pass the tests of your willpower. Situations will arise in life that will test the strength of your will. Many people quit when they face such situations because their willpower is very weak. Your determination to succeed will be tested and you must pass the tests, otherwise, you may quit.

Examples of situations that will test your willpower include:

1. Perspiration

This is a test of hard work. Perspiration is the price success will always demand. You will need to work very hard in order to achieve a purpose. If your willpower is very weak, you will easily quit due to fear of hard work. Sometimes the requirements for success could be so high that only those who are resolute will forge ahead. This is what separates winners from losers. In *2 Kings 2:1-14*, Elisha chased Elijah from Gilgal to the River Jordan in order to receive a double portion of anointing from Elijah. The distance covered on foot by Elisha was over 100 miles. This is a test of hard work and perspiration. It requires strong willpower to pay such price for a goal.

2. Threat.

You may need to overcome threats in order to win. Situations that will threaten you may arise to test your will power. Many people have lost battles due to fear. When fear comes, people surrender and quit. They run for their lives. Only those of strong willpower will not surrender to fear and the enemy's threats.

Acts 4:29
"And now, Lord, behold their threatenings:
and grant unto thy servants, that with all boldness they may
speak thy word."

The disciples faced many threats from the enemies of the gospel, but instead of giving in to fear, they prayed to God for strength. They moved on with their mission and it was accomplished, sometimes at great cost. They demonstrated that their willpower is stronger than any threat and intimidation. Your faith is not yet faith until you are ready to die for it. Don't let fear stop you from winning.

3.   Negative people

You may need to pass the test of negative people. These are the people that speak discouragement into your heart. They don't believe in you. They come to you with a series of bad news stories to discourage you. If your willpower is stronger than any negativity, you will not quit due to bad news.

In **Numbers 13:30-33**, the majority of the Israelite spies became negative about the land they had seen. They claimed that their enemies were stronger than them. Caleb and Joshua had stronger willpower. They maintained their positive position and never joined the rebels. If your willpower is strong, you will not let negative people stop you from your plan.

4.   Mockery

You will need to overcome mockers in order to always win in life. These are the people that celebrate your weaknesses and limitations. They talk badly about you and your work. They laugh at you as you are struggling to win, but very soon, they will be put to shame when you eventually win.

In **Nehemiah 4:3**, enemies mocked Nehemiah, but their mockery could not stop him because his willpower was stronger than any mockery. Nehemiah completed the work and those who made fun of him were defeated. If you can keep yourself busy with your work instead of listening to mockers, they will one day disappear.

5. Negotiation

Your willpower will be tested by the opportunity to drop your plan or exchange it for something else. The world will present before you, another plan or alternative vision. If your willpower is strong enough, you will not negotiate over your plans. You will move on with your purpose.

In **Genesis 25:29-34**, Esau exchanged his birthright for bread and some lentil stew. He failed the test of negotiation and lost the battle of destiny. In **Genesis 39:7-12**, Joseph refused to exchange his destiny for a few minutes of sexual pleasure. He passed the test of negotiation and he excelled in his destiny. If your willpower is strong enough, you will not allow things designed to frustrate your purpose to rule over you.

6. Repeated failure

Failure despite several attempts is a test that you will need to pass if you want to always win in life. It is very possible that you won't get things right at the first attempt, but you must not allow that failure to stop you from trying again and again. In **Mark 5:25**, the ill woman had failed several times in her struggle to find healing. Despite all those failures, when she heard that Jesus was in town, she tried again. Her willpower to get well was stronger than any discouragement. She received her healing. If your willpower is strong enough, you will continue to try until you win.

7. Alertness

This will test the level of your readiness for success. Sometimes, success comes when you least expect it, but your alertness will help you to avoid missing it when it does come.

> *2 Kings 2:10*
> *"And he said, Thou hast asked a hard thing: nevertheless, if thou see me when I am taken from thee, it shall be so unto thee; but if not, it shall not be so."*

Elisha had to pass the test of alertness for him to receive the double portion of anointing he was looking for. Unless he was able to see Elijah at the point of his departure, his dream would not be fulfilled. His strong willpower helped him to keep his attention on Elijah, remaining alert, and then, he received his expectation. If you are really serious and passionate about winning, you will always be alert and ready for opportunities. You will not miss your time.

8. Risk-taking

Your conviction that success is achievable will enable you to take any risk and overcome all obstacles in your way. It requires strong willpower to take risks and ignore the potential negative consequences.

> *Esther 4:16*
> *"Go, gather together all the Jews that are present in Shushan, and fast ye for me, and neither eat nor drink three days, night or day: I also and my maidens will fast likewise; and so will I go in unto the king, which is not according to the law: and if I perish, I perish."*

In this story, Esther had to appear before the king without any invitation. Such impudence was illegal, and she was risking a death sentence. But Esther could not wait until the king invited her because the matter was urgent. She took the risk after seeking the face of God, and she won. If your willpower is strong enough, you will be able to take risks despite the possible consequences.

9.   Loneliness

This is a test you will need to pass when nobody believes in you and your dream. If your willpower is strong enough, you will be ready to go it alone. Whether you have supporters or not will not be a factor, provided your willpower is strong enough.

In *1 Samuel 17*, David fought Goliath alone. Nobody believed David could defeat the mighty Goliath, but the boy ignored the fact that he was on his own in the battle. In reality, the only person whose support you need is God, and David believed God was on his side. God is the one you can rely on when everyone else fails you. A person of strong willpower does not quit because of lack of human support.

10. Crises

Crises can distract you and shift your focus away from your goal. They will severely test your willpower. Sometimes your vision could be a threat to the devil and all his cohorts, such that they will raise different sources of opposition and cause a series of crises in different areas of your life. The plan is to stop you from pursuing your vision. They have seen that if you succeed, your victory will have positive consequences for God's kingdom and negative results for theirs. They are afraid of your success.

If your willpower is strong enough, you will hold on to your vision irrespective of the crises that life throws at you. Marital, financial or any other form of crisis will not put an end to your struggle if your willpower is strong enough. You will need to pass the test of crises to record victory in certain situations of life.

- 7 -

Counsel that Wins

Wise counsel comes from the Word of God and if it is fully observed, there will be victory. This chapter contains a series of insights from the Word of God to help you become a perpetual winner in life. Study and meditate on this counsel and you will gain strength to always be a winner.

1. GO DEEPER

> **Luke 5:4**
> *"Now when he had left speaking, he said unto Simon, Launch out into the deep, and let down your nets for a draught."*

Jesus told Peter to go deeper into the sea for a catch. They had toiled all night with no success. But when they obeyed, they caught an abundance of fish. When situations go wrong for you, instead of giving up, go deeper. Put in more effort, do more research into why you keep on failing, invest more resources and try something new. Don't quit because you failed; instead, increase your effort.

2. SEE THE REWARDS

These are the rewards awaiting you on the other side if you win. Let them motivate you not to quit. Imagine how your life will be transformed if you win. Imagine how many lives you will be able to touch. The fight for victory is worth it.

1 Samuel 17:25-27

"And the men of Israel said, Have ye seen this man that is come up? Surely to defy Israel is he come up: and it shall be, that the man who killeth him, the king will enrich him with great riches, and will give him his daughter, and make his father's house free in Israel. And David spake to the men that stood by him, saying, What shall be done to the man that killeth this Philistine, and taketh away the reproach from Israel? For who is this uncircumcised Philistine, that he should defy the armies of the living God? And the people answered him after this manner, saying, So shall it be done to the man that killeth him."

David saw the gains awaiting him if he won. To David, all the risk was worthy, considering what was at stake. Before you engage in any endeavour, work out what the benefits would be and use them for motivation.

3. JUST FOR TODAY

Avoid building a cloud of concerns about tomorrow in your heart. It will not allow your mind to function very well. It is good for you to live for today. Have concern only for today and leave the future in God's hands.

Matthew 6:11

"Give us this day our daily bread."

> **Psalm 118:24**
> *"This is the day which the LORD hath made; we will rejoice and be glad in it."*

Rejoice in today and trust God for tomorrow. If you can win today, you will win tomorrow. Avoid trying to win the battle of tomorrow when you have not even won that of today. That's not to say that you shouldn't make plans for the future, but don't trust in them – trust in God.

4. YOU CAN WIN

> **1 Corinthians 10:13**
> *"There hath no temptation taken you but such as is common to man: but God is faithful, who will not suffer you to be tempted above that ye are able;*
> *but will with the temptation also make a way to escape, that ye may be able to bear it."*

God will not let you face a battle you can't win. God will not let obstacles come across your path that you can't overcome. That mountain facing you is surmountable and that is why God allows it in your life. You have no excuse for failure. God knows what He has invested in you before He decides to allow you to face those challenges in your life. You can win.

5. ANOINTED FROM BIRTH

> **Jeremiah 1:5**
> *"Before I formed thee in the belly I knew thee; and before thou camest forth out of the womb I sanctified thee, and I ordained thee a prophet unto the nations."*

This verse states that you have been ordained before birth. You were ordained to win in life. The Lord has empowered you to live a life that wins before you were born into this world. That is, you had all it would take to win the battle even before the battle came into existence. You are an ordained winner. Keep on winning!

6. YOU ARE NOT ALONE

Isaiah 43:2
"When thou passest through the waters, I will be with thee; and through the rivers, they shall not overflow thee: when thou walkest through the fire, thou shalt not be burned; neither shall the flame kindle upon thee."

God has promised that He will always be with you in all situations of life. This implies that you will not fight your battle alone. The Lord will always be on your side. If God is on your side, nobody can be against you. You have a companion in battle that is not defeatable.

7. THE MIND-SET OF MIRACLE

1 Samuel 17:40
"And he took his staff in his hand, and chose him five smooth stones out of the brook, and put them in a shepherd's bag which he had, even in a scrip; and his sling was in his hand: and he drew near to the Philistine."

David defeated mighty Goliath using an ordinary stone. David refused to use the armour of King Saul but chose stones. What was going on in his mind to consider a few stones as effective weapons to use against the well-equipped and experienced Goliath? That is the mind of a miracle.

David had totally shifted his mind from the natural to the supernatural. When the supernatural takes over a matter, any weapon is good enough to record victory. Human wisdom said David needed a sword, shield and armour, but God's wisdom in David told him that he would never defeat the giant in a conventional, close-up battle. God knew the way to win was from a distance with a shepherd's missile, out of range of Goliath's sword or spear. David followed God's promptings in his heart, and won.

Develop the mind of the miraculous. Believe that something unusual will happen in your favour as you engage the enemy in battle, because God is on your side. Those resources in your hand are more than enough for victory when God takes over. Don't let your inadequacies deceive you into quitting. Rely on God's adequacy.

8. GOD LOVES YOU

Psalm 16:10
"For thou wilt not leave my soul in hell; neither wilt thou suffer thine Holy One to see corruption."

The love God has towards you will not let Him leave you alone in your battle. He will not let you be put to shame because He loves you. God will not watch the enemy defeat you. If you can arise against your enemy and engage him in battle, your God will intervene for your sake. God has been waiting for you for a long time to challenge the enemy's oppression in your life. Don't be afraid, because God will not let the desire of your enemy prevail.

9. KEEP ON KNOCKING

Luke 11:9-10
"And I say unto you, Ask, and it shall be given you; seek, and ye shall find; knock, and it shall be opened unto you. For every one that asketh receiveth; and he that seeketh findeth; and to him that knocketh it shall be opened."

Sustain your effort. Keep on fighting until you win. Keep up the fight until your have victory. Those who refuse to quit will win and one day they shall sing songs of victory. The first attempt may not yield the desired result but after several attempts, the result will definitely come.

10. DO NOT JUSTIFY FAILURE

Whatever may be the reason for the first failed attempt, don't accept it as the reason not to try again. Never accept the justification for failure; otherwise, it will paralyse your creative ability. If you refuse to be defeated by the reasons for failure, but instead use them as an incentive to find out how to overcome them, you will open up your understanding for invention, new ideas and another strategy to fight again.

In **Numbers 13:30-33**, all the exaggerations of the ten spies could not make Caleb and Joshua to accept that their enemies were undefeatable. They refused to accept the justification for defeat.

11. AVOID REGRET

When situations don't seem to go as you had envisaged, avoid regret. When it seems as if you have made mistakes, avoid regret.

Learn from your mistakes but never allow them to rule your future plan. Regret is an enemy of victory. It creates fear of trying again. Avoid it.

> ### Romans 8:28
> *"And we know that all things work together for good to them that love God, to them who are the called according to his purpose."*

All things that will work together for your good include mistakes, errors, attacks, evil plots and whatever comes your way as you pass through situations. Maintain hope, not regret. Leave the unknowns for God to handle.

12. CHECK YOUR VIEWS CONTINUALLY

A situation may not be as difficult as you perceive it to be. You may soon discover that your opponents are not as strong as you thought. Ensure that you continually put your views and observations under scrutiny. You may be genuinely wrong. Ask mature Christians for their opinions, and ask yourself the reason why you hate what you hate and why you like what you like. Sometimes the flesh can make you see fear where there is no fear.

> ### Psalms 53:5
> *"There were they in great fear, where no fear was: for God hath scattered the bones of him that encampeth against thee: thou hast put them to shame, because God hath despised them."*

Check out your views. You may be operating under an illusion.

13. CHECK YOUR FOCUS

Whatever you focus on will grow. If you focus on a problem too much, it will start appearing bigger to you.

> ### Numbers 13:33
> *"And there we saw the giants, the sons of Anak, which come of the giants: and we were in our own sight as grasshoppers, and so we were in their sight."*

The Israelite spies focused on the size of the Anaks, and as they did so, they grew taller in their imagination, like giants in their sight. Whatever you focus on grows. Focus on God and you will see Him as more than enough in your imagination.

14. IGNORE HUMAN OPINION

Whenever you make an attempt to improve your life or rise against what has been oppressing you, expect people to talk. Some will come with a series of negative opinions. You will need to ignore them and maintain your focus.

Hear the opinions of wise Christians who want to help you improve your life, but shut out the views of the naysayers, pessimists and cynics.

When people started talking against the vision of Nehemiah in **Nehemiah 4**, Nehemiah ignored them. He maintained his focus and completed the job.

- 8 -

Before the Winning Formula

In **Exodus 5:1-23** Moses confronted Pharaoh, as instructed by God, to demand the release of Israel. This was the first time Moses appeared before Pharaoh to make such a demand. The outcome wasn't good. Pharaoh increased the bondage of Israel and made their lives more miserable. The reaction of the Israelites was very negative towards Moses. Moses asked God why He had sent him to do this job, if it was only going to make things worse.

The first failed attempt to overcome a problem is often the most difficult to get over. In Moses' case, this was because the negative outcome was never expected. He wasn't prepared for the fact that victory might not come easily. But if you are able to overcome the disappointment of your first failed attempt, you will be able to move on and overcome whatever that stands in your way. You will be able to overcome all other failed attempts, until you win.

It is always good for you to control your expectations as you attack the operation of the enemy in any area of your life.

Exodus 3:19-20
"And I am sure that the king of Egypt will not let you go, no, not by a mighty hand. And I will stretch out my hand, and smite Egypt with all my wonders which I will do in the midst thereof: and after that he will let you go."

This verse shows that God had warned Moses that he should control his expectations because the deliverance would not come at the first attempt. The deliverance would definitely happen, but not straight away. Therefore, continued application of effort is needed for victory to be secured.

You must understand that in every battle, to set yourself free from the captivity of the oppressor, continual effort will be required.

WRONG RESPONSES TO FAILURE

The common mistakes people make when they encounter their first failed attempt include the following:

1.   They accept failure as the final outcome

Some people think after their first failure that failure is the only possible outcome. They don't realise that their struggle has only just begun. They think that there's no point in carrying on because the outcome will be the same each time. This is wrong.

2.   They start predicting failure

Because they have failed once, they make themselves prophets of doom that predict failure again. Unfortunately, if they start predicting failure in future attempts they will lose courage and resolve, and their prediction will almost certainly come true. There is power in the tongue.

3.   They get used to failure

They start conditioning their lives to accept failure concerning that issue. They adjust their lives to accommodate the challenge or problem. Never get used to failure. Never accept that you will always fail however many times you try.

4. They listen to those that doubt them

When a person fails in his attempt to gain deliverance, those who hear about it start doubting the person's ability to achieve victory. They lose confidence in his efforts. Unfortunately, the person sometimes then listens to those doubters and believes them. Never listen to mockers who doubt your capability.

5. They develop self-pity

Failure opens the door for the devil to attack your mind with self-pity. He will try to make you see yourself as an unfortunate person and to pity yourself for passing through life with such difficulties. Avoid thoughts of self-pity – you can become more comfortable with having a 'pity party' about failure than keeping up the battle for victory. Don't accept that you will spend the rest of your days with your difficulties. Victory is coming very soon, if you don't quit.

6. They change their confession

People make positive confessions before their first attempt at victory, but change their confession when failure seems to prove them wrong. Do not allow the devil to put a different song in your mouth. Do not change your good confession because of the failed attempt. Keep on declaring to the situation that your God is good. Soon, He will show Himself strong on your behalf.

7. They abandon the good fight

It is good to rise against the enemy of your soul. It is right to launch an attack against the situations that make your life miserable. Unfortunately, some people stop fighting at the first sign of failure. Do not abandon the good fight. If you do, the enemy will increase his attacks on your life.

8. They consider their limitation as the sole reason for their failure

Some people strongly believe that it was solely their own weakness that made them fail, forgetting that even the strongest among the strong men encounter failure from time to time. There are also circumstances that can be completely beyond our control, so failure is not our fault. While it is possible for the limitations of your life to contribute to your failure, there are other factors that cause defeat. Sometimes, people fail simply because their time for victory has not come – only God knows when it's the right time for us. Some failures could be due to a premature attack on the enemy, while others might be a matter of God's timing of events. Whatever happens, do not stop fighting your enemy until you get total victory.

9. They stop trusting God

A failure is only a defeat when it depletes faith. When some people fail at their first attempt, despite all the prayers and faith, they have put into it, they stop trusting God. They think that God is not interested in their cause, or even that He isn't real. The question is: how can not trusting in God give you the victory you desire? God never fails. He is not a man; he doesn't have limitations. God will do what He has promised in His time, irrespective of the magnitude of the challenges or the strength of your adversary.

10. They start walking by sight instead of faith

Failure is usually due to certain negative occurrences. The common mistake is that people who have failed start, unknowingly, focusing on the appearances of the events. They become carnal and view the situation from the physical perspective instead of the spiritual perspective. They drift away from faith. They start trusting the natural at the expense of the supernatural. Do not stop walking by faith.

11. They start murmuring

Failure produces anger and annoyance. The disappointment of the first failed attempt can make a person start murmuring – complaining – about both man and God. This action is very provoking to both man and God. The more you complain, the more you make God angry and the more you are far away from success. Do not murmur.

12. They stop interpreting the situation in God's way

Failure can make a person start interpreting the situation in line with the words of men instead of the Word of God. If you allow failure to gain control of your mind, you may see yourself interpreting the situation outside of the Word of God.

13. They become afraid to try again

Failure can generate such fear that the person becomes afraid of trying again. Do not let the enemy threaten you when you want to try again.

14. They lose their virtues

Failure can take away a person's virtues, because discouragement weakens the resolve to be good, to behave well. A good habit is a virtue; don't let failure steal it from you. Maintain your good habits and very soon they will yield good results. Avoid being negative.

15. They lose their self-esteem

Failure will attempt to give you a wrong identity. It will try to make you see yourself wrongly. Do not accept that you are a failure. Do not let the enemy use failure to describe you. Believe in who God says you are, not what the enemy would like you to think you are.

16. They enter into blame game

The devil can make you start considering people around you to be responsible for your failure. This is his attempt to take advantage of your situation to create enmity between you and your Christian brothers and sisters or family or friends. Avoid bitterness and blaming others for what went wrong. Get convinced that when your time comes, nobody can frustrate it.

17. They think their failure means God doesn't love them

A common mistake is to allow your failed attempt to damage your belief in the love of God towards you. God is bigger than your challenges and He has loved you before your problems came into existence. Nothing you can do will make Him love you less, because you are His child and His love is perfect and unchanging.

Your present battle has nothing to do with whether God loves you or not. Your situation is a passing phase of your life. Whether you win now or later, God still loves you. The greatest indicator that reveals God's love towards you is the fact that He allowed His only begotten Son (Jesus) to die for your salvation. That single act of God is greater than any situation of your life.

18. They 'close the gates' of their ears

When people fail, they decide not to listen to any wise counsel or inspiration of the Holy Spirit again; they fear it will lead them to failure again. They think they have done all that could be done, with no results. They believe that there is nothing left for them to do that they have not already done. This is deception. There is often a new thing to try that we have not tried before. But whether that's the case or not, victory in life is not just determined by doing what needs to be done.

Ecclesiastes 9:11

"I returned, and saw under the sun, that the race is not to the swift, nor the battle to the strong, neither yet bread to the wise, nor yet riches to men of understanding, nor yet favour to men of skill; but time and chance happeneth to them all."

This verse shows that there are other hidden factors that determine the winner in the battle of life. Sometimes, circumstances can turn against someone, with unexpected consequences, however, if you do not close the 'gates of your ears', you will discover those hidden factors or be led to the place where the circumstances change.

DEALING WITH FAILURE

If you can handle your first failed attempts properly, you will be able to convert your failure into a stepping stone to success. If you refuse to let failure defeat your determination to succeed, you will have victory after defeat.

Here are some important tips on how to handle failure:

1. Mind your words

There is a possibility of emotional imbalance after failure. Your flesh will attempt to take control of your mouth, so that you start speaking negative words after failure. You must refuse to allow your mouth to speak negative words. Your words will determine the chances of success after failure. There is power in the spoken word. If you continue to speak negatively into your situation after failure, you will complicate the matter and open the door to demonic manipulation of your situation. Mind your words. If you have nothing positive to say after failure, just keep quiet.

2.   Renew your mind

Failure stains the mind. The stains could be the imagination of future failure, the thought that your situation is impossible to overcome, or being overwhelmed with the sorrow of disappointment. Remembrance of past failed efforts could cause the mind to start malfunctioning and generate negative thoughts. You will need to quickly renew your mind by clearing it of any form of stains. Refocus your thought on the possibilities, not the problems, and deny your mind any chance of making you look into the future with hopelessness.

3.   Be calm

Failure causes agitation of the mind and the spirit. It could lead to restlessness and loss of inner peace and joy. Be calm. Calmness paves the way for the inspiration of the Holy Spirit. It allows divine light to shine onto your mind and into your spirit. When you fail, it is not time to talk carelessly or become agitated. It is time to wait for the inspiration of the Holy Spirit about the way forward. Remember that peace of mind is a necessary prerequisite for the Holy Spirit to operate on your situation. *"Be still, and know that I am God..." **(Psalm 46:10)**.*

4. Encourage yourself in the Lord

Failure causes discouragement. You will need to recall the goodness of God in your life in the past. Think about how God has given you victories before. Do not just focus on the present negative situation. Focus on the good old days and the joys you have known. Exploit the victory God has given you in the past to motivate yourself for the future. Do not wait for the people who are aware of your struggle to come and encourage you, lift yourself up and assure yourself that there is blessing in your future. Tell yourself that as long as there is life, there is hope.

5. Take responsibility for the situation

The common mistake, when there is failure, is to start blaming people around you and make them responsible for the failure. Take responsibility for whatever happened. Do not look for somebody else to blame for your failure. If you can take responsibility for the situation, you will be able to look inward and assess your own actions and involvement, so that you can do better next time.

6. Approach God

When you encounter failure, go to God for direction. God knew ahead of time that you would fail, so He is expecting you to come to Him as your Father. The secret of success is in the hand of God and He reveals it to whoever He has chosen. For you to qualify for such divine direction, you will need to approach God with humility. Humble yourself in the hand of God and He will lift you up. Do not blame God for letting you down. Do not ask Him why He has allowed you to fail. He always has good reasons. Trust Him. What is important is the way forward.

7. Release the burden of failure to Jesus

Failure can be a burden – load on your back that can weigh you down. The wisest thing to do is to release that burden into the hands of Jesus. You can do this by giving it over to Jesus in prayer, letting Him take it from you. Lose yourself in praise and worship to him, so that you can even rejoice over that failure. This will release you from carrying the burden of failure around. Do not take on false guilt – it is not a sin to fail (unless your failure was giving in to temptation, of course, in which case the right route is repentance and receiving forgiveness). The consequence of relinquishing the burden is inner joy that flows like a river. Cast your burden onto Jesus and refuse to carry around the concern about what has happened, *"casting all your care upon him; for he careth for you"* **(1 Peter 5:7)**.

8. Learn from failure

Prayerfully consider lessons you can learn from your failed attempts. Explore every action you have taken and the methods you have adopted. Check for possible reasons why things did not work out well for you. Life is a teacher, and whatever you learn today will make you a better person tomorrow. The purpose of this lesson is to do things better next time, not self-condemnation.

9. Prepare to change

Failure could be a signal that the methods used were not appropriate. It could also be a signal to identify hidden things that hinder victory. There may be a need for a change of approach, methods, policy, strategy and ideology. Get ready to change if the need arises. Do not be rigid. Do not continue to use the same old method that never worked. Try new things for possible success. Failure can also be a lesson that we personally need to change in some way – so learn your lesson well.

10. Analyse and identify

This is an act of bringing to the surface hidden things that determine success. There are things that hinder success and there are things that promote success. Analyse what went wrong, and identify the things that might hinder your success so as to avoid them next time. Also identify things that could promote your success, so that you can do them next time. Similarly, check if you have a blind spot—things you could not see very well that might have frustrated your success. The way to find if you have a blind spot is to ask others if there is anything they see about the situation that you have missed, and ask God to identify anything you have been blind to.

11. Get connected

There are people that might have fought the same battle you are fighting before. If so, they can help you if you can get linked to them. Prayerfully consider who could be of help to you in your struggle.

12. Lean on grace

Failure could make success look impossible. It could also make you feel inadequate and incapable of victory. Failure may make you think the challenge is too great for you. But the grace of God is available. Lean on His grace. When God clothes you with the garment of His grace, you will become too much for your opponents. The grace of God makes the weak say: "I am strong."

13. Press on

To persevere will require forgetting things that are behind and looking to things ahead. Failure is behind, so forget it. Success is ahead, so look forward to it. Refuse to be stagnated by failure. Be determined to move on and never surrender.

14. Take solace in the Word of God

The Word of God has the solution for failure. It has methods of dealing with it. So soak yourself in the comfort of God's Word. With the Word of God, you will be able to deny failure a chance of controlling your next move.

Consider the following word of God:

a. God rewards hard-work

> ### Ruth 2:12
> "The LORD recompense thy work, and a full reward be given thee of the LORD God of Israel, under whose wings thou art come to trust."

God rewards every good effort that is made to glorify His name, including your failures (God looks at the motives of the heart). But your success will glorify God's name, so as you keep on fighting the good fight, one day, God will reward your effort with success. So, do not give up.

b. *God will never stop loving you*

Romans 8:38-39
"For I am persuaded, that neither death, nor life, nor angels, nor principalities, nor powers, nor things present, nor things to come, nor height, nor depth, nor any other creature, shall be able to separate us from the love of God, which is in Christ Jesus our Lord."

Failure could create the wrong thought that you failed because God has rejected you and that He hates you. No – God will love you for ever. He will never reject His own people. Whatever happens, assure yourself that God loves you and that He will work all things out for your good *(Romans 8:28)*.

c. *God will not allow you to suffer beyond what you can bear*

1 Corinthians 10:13
"There hath no temptation taken you but such as is common to man: but God is faithful, who will not suffer you to be tempted above that ye are able; but will with the temptation also make a way to escape, that ye may be able to bear it."

God is good. Whatever God allows in your life, it is because you can handle it. God allows it because He foreknew that you can defeat that problem of your life. You have what it takes to win that battle. You have no excuse to quit. Keep on trying until you win.

d. *You have what it takes to win*

Philippians 4:13
"I can do all things through Christ which strengtheneth me."

The source of your strength is not in yourself, but in Christ Jesus. There is no battle you can't win. There is no mountain too big for you to climb. You can do all things. You can win this battle, if you refuse to surrender.

e. You are stronger than you think

Exodus 7:1
"And the LORD said unto Moses, See, I have made thee a god to Pharaoh: and Aaron thy brother shall be thy prophet."

After a series of excuses from Moses about his weaknesses, God told him that he would be a god to his enemy. God made it known to Moses that he was stronger than he thought. He is no more the Moses that he used to be to Pharaoh. He is now a god to Pharaoh. Pharaoh may not realise that, but it doesn't matter; it is the final result that will prove it. You are also a god to your problem. You do have power over it, because you have God's power living inside you. It is your problem that should be afraid of you, not the other way round.

f. You are not fighting alone

Isaiah 43:2
"When thou passest through the waters, I will be with thee; and through the rivers, they shall not overflow thee: when thou walkest through the fire, thou shalt not be burned; neither shall the flame kindle upon thee."

God is always fighting alongside of you. Whether you win or lose, you are in it together with God. If you fail, it's because God has good reasons to allow it. If you can keep fighting, irrespective of the failures, you will soon testify to God's support.

g. You will surely win

> ### Jeremiah 29:11
> "For I know the thoughts that I think toward you, saith the LORD, thoughts of peace, and not of evil, to give you an expected end."

God has promised that He will give you the result that is in His thoughts – the end always turns out as He expects it to. He is not surprised by anything. He will help you to achieve your desire. It is only a matter of time: victory is coming. You will surely win.

h. It is a matter of timing

> ### Ecclesiastes 3:1
> "To every thing there is a season, and a time to every purpose under the heaven…"

> ### Ecclesiastes 3:6
> "A time to get, and a time to lose; a time to keep, and a time to cast away…"

There is a time and a season for everything on this earth. There is a time to experience failure and there will be time to experience victory. Times of failure usually come ahead of that victory. If you can be steadfast in battle, you will experience the time to win. Change is coming to you.

i. It is not only about competency

> **Ecclesiastes 9:11**
>
> *"I returned, and saw under the sun, that the race is not to the swift, nor the battle to the strong, neither yet bread to the wise, nor yet riches to men of understanding, nor yet favour to men of skill; but time and chance happeneth to them all."*

Victory in life is not only about the strength and capabilities of man. Do not blame yourself for your limitations or errors that might have denied you victory. Learn from your error and improve yourself as much as you have opportunity, and then keep on fighting until you win.

j. Divine mercy

> **Romans 9:16**
>
> *"So then it is not of him that willeth, nor of him that runneth, but of God that sheweth mercy."*

It is not only about your ability but also the mercy of God. When the mercy of God comes into operation, the failed person of yesterday will win today. Put your hope in the mercy of God for future victory.

k. Keep on moving

> **Luke 9:5**
>
> *"And whosoever will not receive you, when ye go out of that city, shake off the very dust from your feet for a testimony against them."*

Jesus told His disciples not to wait outside a closed door, but to keep on moving. If one door refuses to open, there are plenty of other doors waiting to open. Keep on moving. If you do not succeed today, tomorrow is still there. If today does not bring you the victory you desire, tomorrow will do.

l. Be among the witnesses

Hebrews 12:1
"Wherefore seeing we also are compassed about with so great a cloud of witnesses, let us lay aside every weight, and the sin which doth so easily beset us, and let us run with patience the race that is set before us..."

There are people whose lives have proved that winning is possible, irrespective of the number of defeats. There are testimonies of people who failed many times before they won. Your situation is not new. If those people could succeed after many attempts, you also can succeed. Let your name be among those that succeed, regardless of the number of failed attempts. Be among the witnesses.

m. Never stop rising

Proverbs 24:16
"For a just man falleth seven times, and riseth up again: but the wicked shall fall into mischief."

God wants you to win. He does not want you to remain defeated. Never stop getting up, dusting yourself off and trying again after your failure. One day, you will get up and never fall again.

n. *Your case is not unusual*

1 Peter 5:9
"Whom resist stedfast in the faith, knowing that the same afflictions are accomplished in your brethren that are in the world."

There is nothing new under heaven. There is nothing happening to you that have never happened to people before. You are not the first to be in such challenges of life. Your case is not strange. There are many other people facing the same situations you're facing today. There are also many people facing worse situations than yours. You will soon have testimonies as other people in your situations have had. Keep on trying and keep on fighting the enemy of your soul. Victory is certain. You are a winner.

- 9 -

The Winning Formula

As I have said often in this book, in many situations of life, victory comes only after many tries. You won't always win at the first attempt; you may need to make several efforts.

The good news is that every seemingly failed attempt you make has an impact on the matter. Though, the mountain of a problem can seems as if it's not moving, something hidden is going on inside the mountain. If you can continue battering away, the mountain will crack. You will soon be amazed at how the situation that once proved unconquerable bows to your blow. It is always the last straw that breaks the camel's back.

If you continue praying, victory might come with your very next prayer. If you make yet another effort, it may be the last you need to make for the problem to be solved. But if you give up, you may never see that victory. If you can endure and maintain the effort, you will see that last straw bring the camel to its knees. That will be your winning formula.

You see, your winning formula is that last blow you strike on your stubborn challenge that makes it bow to your commands. Your winning formula could be that last demand you make for your rights in an organisation that would yield the result despite several previous refusals. Or it could be that last job application you submitted to an employer that will bring you a job, despite all the failed applications and interviews of the past. There is always a last time for an effort to be made that will produce the desired result.

> ### James 4:7
> *"Submit yourselves therefore to God. Resist the devil, and he will flee from you."*

This verse encourages you to keep on trying until your adversary surrenders. Your enemy does not have unlimited strength because he is not God. The power behind your problem is not unbreakable because it is not of God. Those who are making your life miserable don't have all the power. They have limitations. Continual effort from you will push them to their limit and then, they will surrender. With God on your side, you can outrun any competitor. With God on your side, you are stronger than any enemy, whether spiritual or physical.

CASE STUDY

Pharaoh versus Moses

> ### Exodus 5:1-2
> *"And afterward Moses and Aaron went in, and told Pharaoh, Thus saith the LORD God of Israel, Let my people go, that they may hold a feast unto me in the wilderness. And Pharaoh said, Who is the LORD, that I should obey his voice to let Israel go? I know not the LORD, neither will I let Israel go."*

In this story, Moses demanded that Pharaoh let Israel go, but the king refused. In fact, Pharaoh not only refused their demand but also made their slavery worse, to dissuade them from ever demanding freedom again. After this, God did many miracles and brought nine plagues on the Egyptians, yet Pharaoh still refused to let the people of God go. The situation seemed hopeless, as if it would never change. But the reality was that Pharaoh and his people were getting sick and tired of Moses' demands for freedom and the plagues.

Exodus 12:29-33

"And it came to pass, that at midnight the LORD smote all the firstborn in the land of Egypt, from the firstborn of Pharaoh that sat on his throne unto the firstborn of the captive that was in the dungeon; and all the firstborn of cattle. And Pharaoh rose up in the night, he, and all his servants, and all the Egyptians; and there was a great cry in Egypt; for there was not a house where there was not one dead. And he called for Moses and Aaron by night, and said, Rise up, and get you forth from among my people, both ye and the children of Israel; and go, serve the LORD, as ye have said. Also take your flocks and your herds, as ye have said, and be gone; and bless me also. And the Egyptians were urgent upon the people, that they might send them out of the land in haste; for they said, We be all dead men."

This story shows how a stubborn enemy can surrender. The enemy that once portrayed himself as almighty is now defeated. He bowed to the winning formula. He received the blow that broke his courage.

If you are not overwhelmed by the stubbornness of your oppressor, you will soon discover how small his strength is. If you can focus on your God and disregard the apparent strength of your enemy, you will soon rejoice in victory over him.

Who is your Pharaoh?

Your Pharaoh may appear in different forms. He could manifest as:

1. An ignorant oppressor

> ### Exodus 5:2
> *"And Pharaoh said, Who is the LORD, that I should obey his voice to let Israel go? I know not the LORD, neither will I let Israel go."*

Pharaoh was ignorant of the God of Israel – the same God you are serving. He really did not know who God was. If he knew about God, he would not have challenged Him. Do you know that those who are rising against you are ignorant about you? They do not know that you carry the anointing of the Holy Spirit. They do not know about your spiritual strength. Problems in your life have no understanding of who you are – a child of the living God.

The challenges of your life are an opportunity to reveal who you are and what you are made of. When you face a trial in life, consider it an opportunity for you to show to the world that Almighty God is your Father. Until you teach sickness a lesson, it may never respect your authority. Refuse to accept that sickness into your life. Keep on fighting it until it bows. Once it bows, it will never come to you again.

Continue to fight that problem of your life until you overcome it. Once you overcome it, it will never come to you again. If you can keep on fighting that poverty in your life, it will soon learn its lesson, realising that you are stronger than it thought. May God teach your enemy lessons he will never forget, in Jesus' name.

2.   A boastful enemy

Pharaoh was full of boasting. There are many arrogant enemies like him. They boast of their strength, popularity, education, influence, possessions, etc.

Any problem that disobeys the promises of God for your life is your Pharaoh. The Word of God promises that you shall not be barren, yet the spirit of barrenness may be attacking you and resisting every attempt for freedom that you make.

> ### 2 Corinthians 10:4-5
> "(For the weapons of our warfare are not carnal, but mighty through God to the pulling down of strong holds;) Casting down imaginations, and every high thing that exalteth itself against the knowledge of God, and bringing into captivity every thought to the obedience of Christ..."

This Bible verse promises that whatever exalts itself against the knowledge of God in your life can be cast down, if you use the spiritual weapons of Christian warfare. Those situations of your life that defy all solution shall be cast down by God if you ask in fervent prayer. Even your boastful oppressor will soon be cast down and disgraced, if you refuse to bow down to its authority.

> ### Isaiah 41:12
> *"Thou shalt seek them, and shalt not find them, even them that contended with thee: they that war against thee shall be as nothing, and as a thing of nought."*

It is my prayer that whatever represents the enemy in your life shall be taken away by God today, in Jesus' name.

3.   One who questions God

> ### Exodus 5:2
> *"And Pharaoh said, Who is the LORD, that I should obey his voice to let Israel go? I know not the LORD, neither will I let Israel go."*

Pharaoh asked: "Who is that God of Israel?" Your Pharaoh is that situation of your life asking you, "Who is your God?" That is, "Who is your God to deliver you from my hand? Who can stop me from continuing to make your life miserable? Who is able to overcome my control over you?"

The situation of your life asking you these questions is your Pharaoh. That situation questioning the integrity of God in your life is your Pharaoh. That situation that wants to make your God a liar by frustrating God's promises concerning you is your Pharaoh. The good news is that very soon, your God will answer that question by saying: "I am able." God will soon answer your enemy that He will deliver you from his hand.

When the God of Israel shows up, Pharaoh has to surrender.

> **Isaiah 14:27**
> *"For the LORD of hosts hath purposed,*
> *and who shall disannul it? And his hand is stretched out,*
> *and who shall turn it back?"*

Today, God will stretch His hand out into the situation of your life for your sake, in Jesus' name.

4.   A tyrant

Pharaoh was a tyrant. He was an absolute dictator. He lived above any law or regulation. He had the authority to do as he liked with people. He could punish and threaten those he hated.

> **Exodus 5:4**
> *"And the king of Egypt said unto them, Wherefore do ye,*
> *Moses and Aaron, let the people from their works? Get you*
> *unto your burdens."*

Pharaoh made laws without the need for anyone else's approval. He increased the burden on God's people because they demanded their freedom. That person in your life making your life miserable is your Pharaoh. That person who has power to do as he pleases with your life is your Pharaoh. He has made himself your god. He wants you to worship him like an idol. He oppresses your life as he wishes; he makes and unmakes laws as he considers fit.

The good news is that your God will defeat him. Your God is coming to bring that Pharaoh down, as you keep on crying to your God for intervention.

I pray that every wicked person making your life miserable will come under the judgement of God today, in Jesus' name.

5.   A suppressor

Pharaoh directed and restrained the destiny of God's people. He pressed them down mentally, emotionally, psychologically, economically, etc., such that they would not be able to rise again. He was afraid of their prosperity. He was a suppressor.

> ### Exodus 1:9-10
> "And he said unto his people, Behold, the people of the children of Israel are more and mightier than we: Come on, let us deal wisely with them; lest they multiply, and it come to pass, that, when there falleth out any war, they join also unto our enemies, and fight against us, and so get them up out of the land."

These verses show how Pharaoh mobilised all the Egyptians to suppress the Israelites, so that they would not be able to rise in life.

Your Pharaoh is that situation that is pressing you down so that you will not be able to rise. Your colleagues who are plotting against you so that you will not get promoted at work are your Pharaoh. That spirit that is pressing you down so that you will lose the courage to forge ahead in your endeavour is your Pharaoh. The reality is that enemy is afraid of your prosperity, because the more prosperous you are, the more difficult it becomes for him to manipulate your destiny.

Failure and poverty are strong weapons the enemy uses to control the destiny of a man. The good news is that God will soon overthrow whatever is slowing you down both internally and externally. Resist the forces that are trying to suppress your mind, spirit or life. Refuse to be demotivated. Refuse to be stagnant.

6. An oppressor

This is a person who subjects others to undue pressures. He forces fellow human beings to do things against their will.

> ### Exodus 1:11
> "Therefore they did set over them taskmasters to afflict them with their burdens. And they built for Pharaoh treasure cities, Pithom and Raamses."

Pharaoh set taskmasters over the Israelites to make them work against their will. Oppression can come through a human being or directly from a demonic spirit. Evil pressures are intended to force a person to do things he or she would not have done naturally. When you find yourself under pressure to act against your will, the spirit of Pharaoh is at work in your life. If your relatives bring pressure on you to do certain things you consider wrong, the spirit of Pharaoh is at work in your life. You will need to resist that pressure prayerfully.

I pray that every source producing evil pressure upon your life shall dry up today, in Jesus' name.

7. An evil chaser

Satan hates losing his possessions – and wants them back.

> ### Exodus 14:9
> *"But the Egyptians pursued after them, all the horses and chariots of Pharaoh, and his horsemen, and his army, and overtook them encamping by the sea, beside Pihahiroth, before Baalzephon."*

After the deliverance of Israel, Pharaoh and his army chased Israel, intending to return them to slavery. Your Pharaoh is that power or personality running after you for an evil purpose. That power that wants you to lose the job you recently got after many years of joblessness is your Pharaoh. That situation of your life that wants you to lose the blessings you recently received from God is your Pharaoh. That situation of your life that wants to lure you back into your ungodly practises of the past, or back into the unbelief you had before becoming a Christian, is your Pharaoh. Therefore, you will need to confront the Pharaoh that wants to reverse your deliverance.

I pray that you will never return into slavery again, in Jesus' name.

8. An envious person

Pharaoh was very envious, hating the blessing of God on his children. Satan hates our blessings too.

> ### Exodus 1:9
> *"And he said unto his people, Behold, the people of the children of Israel are more and mightier than we."*

Pharaoh was afraid of the prosperity of Israel. He was very envious of their fruitfulness. Envy is a murderous emotion. As

God is blessing you, those that hate you and are wishing you evil are your Pharaoh. They wished you were never blessed. Your blessings provoke them to jealousy. They are your Pharaoh. When God promotes you at work or gives you a pay rise, the colleagues who think they should have got that job or money are your Pharaoh.

Some people think that they should always be ahead of you in life, and if they think that it's the other way round, they are envious. The good news is that the God who gives blessings knows how to protect you against envious people.

May you see the fall of your enemy, in Jesus' name.

9. A stubborn person

Exodus 3:19
"And I am sure that the king of Egypt will not let you go, no, not by a mighty hand."

God had said ahead of time that Pharaoh was going to be very stubborn; he would not obey any command that would not profit him. A stubborn person does not change his mind. When a stubborn person decides to afflict a fellow human being, no external force can persuade him to change his mind unless it is greater than he is. That person in your life that stubbornly pursues you for evil is your Pharaoh. That challenging situation that defies all solution is your Pharaoh. That problem that refuses to depart from your life is your Pharaoh.

The good news is that stubbornness against the children of God by any enemy will cause the destruction of that enemy. The stubbornness of Pharaoh led him to his own destruction. Do not be afraid of any stubborn enemy. God allows it to give that enemy the opportunity to change his or her mind. But when it is very clear that enough opportunities have been given for a change of heart but to no avail, then your God will take that person out of your way.

I pray that every stubborn situation of your life shall come under the judgement of God today, in Jesus' name.

10. A selfish person

Pharaoh was only interested in whatever benefited him. He would do anything to protect his selfish ambition.

> ### Exodus 5:4
> "And the king of Egypt said unto them, Wherefore do ye, Moses and Aaron, let the people from their works? Get you unto your burdens."

Pharaoh did not want to let Israel go because of the wealth he enjoyed from their free services to his kingdom. The Israelites had built treasure cities for Pharaoh that they would never dwell in (Exodus 1:11). Your Pharaoh is the one who resists your freedom for selfish gain. He profits from your slavery. Those that benefit from your wasteful lifestyle or addiction will not be happy when you decide to change. Those that benefit from your prodigal way of life will oppose anything that leads you to repent.

I pray that whoever the devil has planted in your life to promote your enslavement shall be rooted out of your life today in Jesus' name. Any power or personality resisting your freedom shall be broken today, in Jesus' name.

> ### Isaiah 65:22
> *"They shall not build, and another inhabit; they shall not plant, and another eat: for as the days of a tree are the days of my people, and mine elect shall long enjoy the work of their hands."*

11. A manipulator

A manipulator has the ability to influence, manage, use or control situations or people to their own advantage, by direct or indirect means.

> ### Exodus 1:9-10
> *"And he said unto his people, Behold, the people of the children of Israel are more and mightier than we: Come on, let us deal wisely with them; lest they multiply, and it come to pass, that, when there falleth out any war, they join also unto our enemies, and fight against us, and so get them up out of the land."*

Pharaoh used the words "let us" to persuade people see his plan as their own. He demanded support from his people against Israel, for his personal gain as well as the benefit of his people. A manipulator is able to make people rally round him to further his personal goals. He makes people think they are defending their own cause when in fact it his personal cause they are defending. Your Pharaoh is that man gathering support to attack you. He lures people to join him, deceiving them into believing that they are doing it for their own good. Do not be afraid of his evil supporters because they will receive their judgement from God.

They will soon turn against each other. But do be wise to the tactics of manipulators. Watch out for their tricks.

> ### Isaiah 54:15
> *"Behold, they shall surely gather together, but not by me: whosoever shall gather together against thee shall fall for thy sake."*

12. A troublemaker

The children of Israel did not commit any offence that justified Pharaoh's enslavement of them. They were busy focusing on their own business before Pharaoh caused them trouble.

You don't need to offend Pharaoh before he will attack you. Troublemakers like him hate you for no reason – they are your Pharaoh. The challenge that comes into your life through no fault of your own is your Pharaoh. This is not a matter of being wrong but of a troubler at work. A troublemaker brings problems into a peaceful home. The spirit of Pharaoh makes the innocent suffer for sins they have not committed.

When you notice that there is no justification for certain evils that befall you, arise against the spirit of Pharaoh. Avoid self-pity. It is the continual counter attack, prayerfully, on the attacker that brings victory.

May God trouble your troublemaker, in Jesus' name.

13. A child killer

Literally, this is the act of killing infants. The obvious equivalent in our culture is the temptation to abort a child. But there is also a spiritual meaning.

In *Exodus 1:16*, Pharaoh commanded the midwives to kill Hebrew infants that were boys, and the dreams of the future were shattered for thousands of Israelite families. The spirit of Pharaoh likes killing dreams, ideas and visions in their infancy. Why? Because he wants to stop them before they can grow and come to fruition.

This spirit attacks good ideas and plans at the early stage. That spirit or personality that does not want you to start or lay the foundation for a good project is your Pharaoh. The spirit of Pharaoh creates complication at an early stage of a good project to enforce its abandonment. You will need to fight initial challenges whenever you start a new project, because the enemy will attempt to frustrate it.

I pray that every complication awaiting you at the start of a new idea shall fail, in Jesus' name.

14. A captor

Pharaoh captured treasures that belonged to Israel. He took the wealth that was created by their labour. He also captured their peace, joy and freedom through his oppression, and took away their self-esteem.

Your Pharaoh is that power or organisation that has in its possession what belongs to you. The hand that is illegally keeping back your blessings is your Pharaoh. That situation that has taken away your liberty is your Pharaoh. That challenge of your life that has made you lose your self-esteem is your Pharaoh.

Exodus 12:35-36
"And the children of Israel did according to the word of Moses; and they borrowed of the Egyptians jewels of silver,

> and jewels of gold, and raiment: And the LORD gave the
> people favour in the sight of the Egyptians, so that they lent
> unto them such things as they required. And they spoiled
> the Egyptians."

The God of justice worked upon Pharaoh and all the Egyptians, with the result that they paid Israel, in one night, all the wages of the past that they owed them for their years of slavery.

May God arise for your sake and force your Pharaoh to release to you all your possessions in his hand, in Jesus' name. Today, you receive back all your captured benefits. You receive back all your captured joy, peace, self-esteem, etc., in Jesus' name.

15. A demonised attacker

Pharaoh worshipped the Egyptian gods and therefore the demonic spirits behind them. He had occult magicians working for him. This implies that he was under demonic influence against Israel. He had yielded his will to demonic control and he followed their dictates. That demonised enemy of yours is your Pharaoh. That warlock, witchdoctor or witch working against your life is your Pharaoh. That 'Jezebel' spirit raising an attacker against you is your Pharaoh.

Some human enemies operate under the influence of demons. They are very ruthless, devilish and have no compassion for those who are suffering. Your Pharaoh could be that person trying to use demonic spirits to control your destiny and action. The good news is that the Word of God will defeat them when used against their evil schemes.

> **Numbers 23:23**
> "Surely there is no enchantment against Jacob, neither is there any divination against Israel: according to this time it shall be said of Jacob and of Israel, What hath God wrought!"

This verse implies that no evil utterance will work against your destiny, if you are faithful to Christ. No demonised person will succeed against you. You don't need to be afraid of them because all their effort against your life shall come to nothing. The name of Jesus, the blood of Jesus and the Word of God are stronger than any demonic power.

Every evil word spoken into your destiny shall come to nothing, in Jesus' name.

MOSES

Moses took on Pharaoh and prevailed. He demonstrated the attributes of a winner. The life of Moses teaches us the lesson that with certain attributes there is no battle that is too big for a Christian to win. Believe it, your Pharaoh can be defeated.

Moses demonstrated the following attributes that helped him win all his battles.

1. Moses hated enslavement

Moses hated the situation of Israel in Egypt – their bondage. In **Exodus 2:11-12**, he defended an Israelite slave against a brutal Egyptian, although, his anger went too far and he committed murder.

For you to win your battle, you must hate the situation. You are not to hate a human being, but you must not accept the evil that any human being is doing to you. You must hate with a passion, your trouble, obstacle or frustration.

> ### Exodus 34:8
> *"And Moses made haste, and bowed his head toward the earth, and worshipped."*

Moses gave no half-measures in his worship – he was passionate for God. Be a person of passion. Be active in battle. Don't be lukewarm towards the Bible's teaching that will enable you to win.

God will not work for you if you are half-hearted or lukewarm. You must care; you must hate sin and any situation that defies the kingdom of God. When you are passionate about finding a solution and ready to pay any price to find your freedom, God will be ready to act.

2. Moses enjoyed divine fellowship

> ### Exodus 24:18
> *"And Moses went into the midst of the cloud, and gat him up into the mount: and Moses was in the mount forty days and forty nights."*

Moses loved being in the presence of God, fellowshipping with Him. If you love divine fellowship, you will have access to secrets and revelation knowledge that will enable you to win your battles. Be a worshipper. It brings down the presence of God into your situation for victory. In all your battles, keep worshiping God, fellowshipping with Him regularly.

3. Moses made the sacrifice

Hebrews 11:27
"By faith he forsook Egypt, not fearing the wrath of the king: for he endured, as seeing him who is invisible."

Moses knew that he had to ignore all the pleasures of being in the palace of Pharaoh in order to set his people free. He paid the price of victory. You will need to identify prices you have to pay to defeat your enemy. Every success story has a price tag. Be ready to deny yourself certain pleasures in order to have your victory. You may need to reduce the time you spend in bed, reduce your eating intake or deny yourself certain privileges that may hinder you from winning.

4. Moses was a visionary

He was always looking forwards, not backwards *(Hebrews 11:27)*. He looked ahead. He knew that looking backwards would arrest the progress of his life. He saw the Promised Land ahead and he focused on it. You can't have victory unless you look towards it. Avoid looking backwards. You can't have the victory unless you see it by faith. You must see yourself coming out of that problem; otherwise, you will not be able to defeat it.

5. Moses embraced the gains

Moses saw the benefit of fighting for freedom and he loved it. He loved the Promised Land he saw with the 'eyes of the mind'.

> ***Hebrews 11:26***
> *"Esteeming the reproach of Christ greater riches than the treasures in Egypt: for he had respect unto the recompence of the reward."*

Moses saw that freedom is better than bondage and being on your own land is better than living as a tenant. You must embrace the fact that healing is better than sickness, no matter the justification for the sickness, and riches are better than poverty. You must embrace the gains of victory and consider them worth fighting for.

6. Moses endured the shame

He was prepared to suffer the shame (reproach) attached to his cause in order to achieve victory *(Hebrews 11:26)*. You will need to practise the delay of gratification if you are to win. The road to victory could be very rocky and covered with shame. The glory will shine later, but it will be after the victory is won. Ignore all mockery and focus on your cause, and very soon, your mockers will be put to shame.

7. Moses chose rightly

Moses made many decisions during his conflict with Pharaoh, but he got all of them right. The secret of this was based on the fact that Moses was not assuming. He always asked God for direction. You will need to be unassuming. Accept what you don't know and seek those who do know for help.

8. Moses was very bold

Moses never showed fear of Pharaoh, despite knowing how powerful he was. Moses appeared many times before Pharaoh with boldness, despite being a meek person himself. He confronted his oppressor. You will need boldness so that you are not cowered by the empty threats of your enemy. Boldly face your adversary and demand your deliverance. Avoid being intimidated by the situation.

9. Moses was very humble

He covered himself with a garment of humility *(Numbers 12:3)*. Humility will make you teachable. In *Exodus 18:13-24*, Moses accepted the teaching of his father in-law about administration. Humility helped him to be teachable. It will also help you to accept that you don't know what you don't know. Humility helps you to seek help. Be humble, because it will make it easier for people to relate to you and help you

10. Moses paid attention to details

In *Exodus 40:16-17*, Moses completed the tabernacle according to all the information God gave him. Attention to details will help you to win because by it, you will avoid serious errors. What can seem trivial can turn out to be crucial – so don't ignore the small things. If God has commanded it, it's important. You must be able to follow, in detail, instruction or counsel that will give you victory. You must not compromise accuracy. Every piece of relevant information deserves proper consideration. It requires obedience to follow all the instructions in detail, so always walk in obedience.

11. Moses was very forgiving

In many situations, he interceded for those who opposed him. Forgiveness will help you to avoid carrying the load of bitterness

127

through life. Such a load could drag you down and halt the progress in your journey. For you to be able to always win, you must not carry bitterness. Bitterness will hinder your spirit from receiving divine guidance that could give you victory. Be quick to forgive your offender so that you can continue to enjoy divine fellowship with God.

12. Moses was stable

He never wavered in his convictions. He was stable in his decisions and followed them through. Once his mind was made up, he never considered quitting or changing his mind. To win in life, you must be stable in mind, spirit, decisions, emotions, and in all your ways. You can't keep changing your mind after making a decision. Let your 'yes be yes' and 'no be no'. Stop wavering between opinions. Be stable. Be constant.

13. Moses was selfless

He loved people more than himself. He always put people first. On many occasions, Moses interceded for the Israelites before God, because he loved them. Selfishness will rob you of beneficial support from people. There are some battles you can't win alone. You will need people to give you support. The reality is that people withdraw from a selfish person. Walk in love towards people and they will rally round to support you on the day you need their help.

14. Moses knew God's ways

God's ways include His style, method and approach to situations. In *Exodus 33:13*, Moses asked God to show him His ways and God did. After that, Moses always handled situations in God's way (with one notable exception at the end of his life, which meant he saw the Promised Land but couldn't enter it himself). God has His own way of dealing with situations. He has His way of handling enemies of His children. He has His way of blessing His children. You will need to know and apply God's ways to your actions. His ways are found in His Word. Fight in God's way and you will always win.

15. Moses was hungry for more of God

Moses was never satisfied with his spiritual level; he always wanted to know more of God. In **Exodus 33**, Moses asked for God's way and when God showed him, he went further, asking God for more things, even to see God's glory **(verse 18)**. He had a deep hunger for more of God. The more of God you know, the more certain will be your victory. What separates winners from losers is the level of their knowledge about God. Seek for more of God. Keep hungry for more of God. The more God fills you with Himself, the more you should ask for more of Him.

16. Moses knew his limitations

In **Exodus 4**, Moses talked to God about his limitations. You need to know your limitations – what you can take and what you are unable to take. You also need to know your weaknesses – what is in you that is capable of frustrating your destiny. Don't carry more than your ability. Don't expose yourself to situations you can't handle. When you know your limitations, you will know the kind of help you should seek. The understanding of your capabilities will enable you to know what you should not take on, and what to avoid exposing yourself to. Don't fight a battle you have not been trained for. Seek help.

17. Moses knew his enemy

Moses was brought up in the palace of Pharaoh, so he understood his enemy. Moses knew very well who Pharaoh was and how he would react. You should know your enemy. You should understand the strength of your adversary. This will help you to properly plan your strategy and methods. If you are fighting poverty, acquire deep understanding of the problems of poverty. Know your enemy before you rise against it.

18. Moses knew what he wanted

> ### Exodus 8:25
> *"And Pharaoh called for Moses and for Aaron, and said, Go ye, sacrifice to your God in the land."*

Moses was given conditional freedom in this verse. Pharaoh would let the people go and make their sacrifice to God, but only somewhere in Egypt. Moses rejected this. He replied: *"It is not meet so to do; for we shall sacrifice the abomination of the Egyptians to the Lord our God: lo, shall we sacrifice the abomination of the Egyptians before their eyes, and will they not stone us?"* **(Verse 26)**. Moses knew what he wanted – complete freedom to leave Egypt. He knew what he was fighting for.

You must know what you want. Do not accept a conditional victory. Do not accept healing that requires staying on medicines for life – continue to pray for complete healing. Do not accept a job with conditions that will make it impossible for you to carry out the job properly. By faith, you will need to rise up against any evil attachment to your victory, so that you might have total victory.

19. Moses was a good negotiator

In several situations, Moses persuaded God to change His mind or reduce His punishment on the Israelites who rebelled against God. He engaged God in logical argument. Develop the power to negotiate. There may come a time when you need to engage in a discussion that will affect your victory. Avoid dancing to the tune of the opposition. Stick to your own position and clearly state the merit of your case. Let the opposition side realise the superiority of your arguments to theirs. Make your case clear and detailed, with all relevant justification.

20. Moses was very resolute

He was a man of unbreakable spirit. He kept on going to Pharaoh for the liberty of the Israelites until his request was granted. He maintained courage and consistency. He kept on doing the same thing until he obtained the results. He was not defeated by disappointment. The repeated negative responses of Pharaoh failed to deter him from his course. He would not take 'no' for an answer. Be a person of unbreakable spirit. Instead of resorting to self-pity and blame, resolve to maintain your stand until victory comes. Be resolute.

21. Moses created faith and hope

When the Israelites became negative, Moses always calmed them down with words of hope and faith. When all hope seems lost, create more hope for yourself. When it seems as if the enemy is winning, create faith within yourself. Learn how to strengthen yourself in the Lord. When people around you discover that you always walk in faith and hope, they will not have the courage to bring words of doubt and hopelessness to your ear.

22. Moses was well educated

Acts 7:22
"And Moses was learned in all the wisdom
of the Egyptians..."

Moses educated himself. Education brings wisdom that excels. Educate yourself. Read books that will add to your wisdom. Read books written by those who have fought battles of life and won. Empower your thinking ability. Study the Bible and Bible commentaries for better insight. Deep knowledge accelerates victory. There is a lot you can learn in life. Learn from people's experiences, the situations around you, and the testimonies of other people. Read people's success stories. Learn from both the successes and failures of people. The more you know the more the chance of winning in life.

23. Moses spoke prophetically

Exodus 10:28-29
"And Pharaoh said unto him, Get thee from me, take heed
to thyself, see my face no more; for in that day thou seest
my face thou shalt die. And Moses said, Thou hast spoken
well, I will see thy face again no more."

Moses told Pharaoh that he would not see his face again. How this would come to pass Moses did not know, but he said it in faith, and it came true. Moses never saw the face of Pharaoh again.

You must learn how to speak prophetically to your challenges. Speak your heart's desire to your trouble. Tell your adversary that it shall be no more. Rebuke that horrible situation of your life. Let that sickness know that it can no longer stay in your body anymore. Decree an end to your trouble. When you speak prophetically, do not reason the situation out. Do not ask yourself how your prophecy will come to pass. Your responsibility is to utter the words in accordance with the spoken and written Word of God, and then leave the rest for God to handle.

24. Moses had a rod

Exodus 4:2
"And the LORD said unto him, What is that in thine hand? And he said, A rod."

God performed many wonders through the rod of Moses. It ceased to be an ordinary rod when he started his ministry; God started using his rod for miracles. You have a rod in your hand, which God has given you for the days ahead. This was given for the days of battles. Your rod is that small thing in your house that God can use to give you victory over your enemies. Though it appears insignificant, when God takes over, it can do wonders.

Your rod could be a specific word of wisdom God has given you in the past that could give you victory in the battle of today. Your rod could be a friend that God can use to link you to the door of deliverance. Your rod could be a certain person who is interested in you and always ready to give you help when needs arise. Your rod could be some little resource that God can anoint to set you free from poverty. Your rod could be a hidden advantage you have over your adversary that you have yet to discover. You have a rod in your hand. Check it out.

25. Moses was mighty in words

> ### Acts 7:22
> "And Moses... was mighty in words and in deeds."

Moses always spoke with authority. He spoke with assurance, and those who heard his words were convinced that he knew what he was talking about. Moses never spoke as men do. He spoke the anointed Word of God with boldness. His words always came to pass.

To win your battle, you must always speak the Word of God to the situation with boldness. Do not speak the word of man. The word of man has no power and it is always negative and discouraging. Speak the word of life into your dead situation and soon, victory will come. Speak continually to your situation as it is written in the Bible and soon, you will testify. Be mighty in words.

26. Moses was a testifier

> ### Exodus 18:8-9
> "And Moses told his father in law all that the LORD had done unto Pharaoh and to the Egyptians for Israel's sake, and all the travail that had come upon them by the way, and how the LORD delivered them. And Jethro rejoiced for all the goodness which the LORD had done to Israel, whom he had delivered out of the hand of the Egyptians."

Moses gave a good report about God. He testified to the goodness of God. He used his mouth to declare the goodness and faithfulness of God. The mouth that always declares the goodness of God will always have something good from God to declare. Be a testifier. Do not just focus on the present battle of your life. Declare the past victories God has given you. Bring the past into the present situation. Let the enemy know that your God is good to you. Tell the world that the God who delivered you in the past will deliver you again and again. God has made you win before, and He will make you win again.

27. Moses gave God all the glory

Exodus 17:15
"And Moses built an altar, and called the name of it Jehovahnissi..."

Jehovahnissi means 'the Lord our banner'. Moses said it was God who gave them victory, not the strength of their hands. He gave God all the glory. Learn how to give God all the glory in all your successes. The more you give God all the glory, the more you will win in life. Never attribute success to your ability. Acknowledge that God is the giver of victory. This will motivate God to fight for you.

28. Moses was an early riser

Exodus 34:4
"And he hewed two tables of stone like unto the first; and Moses rose up early in the morning, and went up unto mount Sinai, as the LORD had commanded him, and took in his hand the two tables of stone."

Moses rose up early to meet God. Be an early riser. It will give you the opportunity to receive fresh revelation from God to face the new day. While your enemy is busy sleeping, rise up to meet your God. If you spend time with God, you will always be better prepared to overcome the day's troubles and the enemy's attacks.

29. Moses knew that God was with him

Moses knew that the mighty God was always on his side, so he was never afraid of Pharaoh and his capability. To Moses, Pharaoh was nobody. The assurance and conviction that God is always with you creates in you unshakable confidence to face challenges. Your mind will remain focused without a single iota of fear. Even if no one else is with you, you will still win because God is with you. God is with you and He is for you. You can't be defeated because God is on your side.

30. Moses was a fighter

A fighter makes the first move. He initiates a battle against his opponents. A fighter fights for a cause. He has justification for fighting. Moses was the first to start the battle against Pharaoh. He was the first to declare war on Pharaoh. He entered the palace of Pharaoh to demand freedom for Israel. He did not wait for Pharaoh to free Israel because he knew that would never happen. He made the first move. He was justified in approaching Pharaoh for freedom, because it is wrong to enslave people. Be a fighter. Do not wait for a certain problem to depart from your life on its own accord, because it may never happen. Make the first move. Rise against that challenge in your life. Be an attacker, not a defender. There are certain problems that will never willingly leave your life unless you rise against them.

VICTORY AT LAST!

Exodus 12:29-33

"And it came to pass, that at midnight the LORD smote all the firstborn in the land of Egypt, from the firstborn of Pharaoh that sat on his throne unto the firstborn of the captive that was in the dungeon; and all the firstborn of cattle. And Pharaoh rose up in the night, he, and all his servants, and all the Egyptians; and there was a great cry in Egypt; for there was not a house where there was not one dead. And he called for Moses and Aaron by night, and said, Rise up, and get you forth from among my people, both ye and the children of Israel; and go, serve the LORD, as ye have said. Also take your flocks and your herds, as ye have said, and be gone; and bless me also. And the Egyptians were urgent upon the people, that they might send them out of the land in haste; for they said, We be all dead men."

Moses' enemy surrendered willingly, in the end. Pharaoh, a very stubborn enemy, finally caved in. He accepted defeat. The pressure became unbearable. Moses' winning formula from God inevitably defeated Pharaoh. The final blow is in the hand of God. Only God knows the secret of your enemy. Only God knows what will make your adversary surrender.

Pharaoh received many blows in the fight − all the plagues that God sent − but he was still maintaining his position, until the last plague. Only God knew the limit of his strength. Every problem of your life has limited strength. If you can keep on fighting, you will soon wear your enemy down. If you refuse to give up, God will continue fighting for you. As long as you don't surrender, God will drag the situation to its limit, to the point where it will surrender to your will.

May God give you a courage that can't be defeated. May God make you stronger than your adversary, in Jesus' name.

- 10 -

Prayer that Wins

Father, you are a man of war, fight all my battles for me, in Jesus' name.

Father, arise and overthrow all the machineries and weapons of the enemy in operation against my life, in Jesus' name.

I destroy every stumbling block and hindrance on my way to victory, and I use the blood of Jesus to overcome all the enemies of my good testimonies, in Jesus' name.

Father, silence any power, personality or spirit that wants to silence me and dissolve every demonic threat against my destiny in Jesus' name.

I use the blood of Jesus to wipe off every mark of failure and defeat in all areas of my life, in Jesus' name.

Every evil prophecy of defeat spoken into my life by any tongue is nullified, in Jesus' name.

Father, let every evil hand fashioned against my victory wither, in Jesus' name.

Father, destroy whatever in me that will attract evil and break any link between me and any evil agent. Let every evil plan designed against my life die today, in Jesus' name.

Father, restore unto me all my wasted opportunities and give me double for all my lost blessings, in Jesus' name.

Father, let the wickedness of the wicked be terminated in all areas of my life and rebuke the devourer for my sake, in Jesus' name.

Father, strengthen my prayer altar and destroy every demonic attack against my prayer life, in Jesus' name.

Father, anoint me with fresh oil and move me from strength to strength, in Jesus' name.

Father, by your grace, let me run and not be weary and help me to walk and not faint, in Jesus' name.

Father, mark me for protection, favour and honour. Position me for success in all my endeavours, in Jesus' name.

Father, arise and trouble my troubler. Make me to dwell in a perfect peace and let no man trouble me and all that is mine, in Jesus' name.

Father, anoint me with the spirit of wisdom and revelation and let me be always ahead of any evil competitor, in Jesus' name.

Father, because you are with me, let no man be able to stand against me all the days of my life, in Jesus' name.

Father, because you are with me, let my enemies become your enemies, and let my battle become your battle, in Jesus' name.

Every limitation the foundation of my life has put on my destiny be destroyed now, in Jesus' name. I refuse to be limited in life, in Jesus' name.

Holy Spirit, may your fire burn through me and destroy every remnant of the work of the enemy in all areas of my life, in Jesus' name.

Whatever in my life is advertising evil, fire of God destroys it today, in Jesus' name.

Whatever in my life that is praising the devil, fire of God destroys it today, in Jesus' name.

Father, whatever in my life that contradicts the beauty of your glory, is removed today, in Jesus' name.

Father, replace those who are helping me to manage my problems with those who will take me out of my problems, in Jesus' name.

Father, build an army of helpers for me. Surround me with destiny builders, in Jesus' name.

Father, let those who have witnessed my shame also witness my honour. Make me a wonder to the world, in Jesus' name.

Father, arise and overthrow any evil kingdom or throne in operation in any area of my life. Establish your dominion in all areas of my life, in Jesus' name.

Father, if I have become my own problem in any way, deliver me today, in Jesus' name.

Every crooked path in the journey of my life, Father, straightens it today, in Jesus' name.

Father, whatever needs to be sanctified in me for me to possess my possessions, sanctify it today, in Jesus' name.

Father, henceforth, whenever I walk in, let defeat and failure walk out. Create a wall of separation between my life and that of defeat and failure, in Jesus' name.

Father, let all the plans and designs of defeat be destroyed in all areas of my life, in Jesus' name.

Father, whatever battle needs to be won for my life to bring glory and honour to your name, fight it for me today, in Jesus' name.

I tear down, by faith, every wall of separation between me and my victory, in Jesus' name.

Father, I thank you, for you will not only make me win but also make me reign in life by your Spirit, in Jesus' name.

BOOKS FROM THE SAME AUTHOR

Journey to the Next Level

The New Creature

Building a Glorious Home:
A Pathway to a Successful Marriage

Words that Heal

This book, and all other books from the same author, are available at Christian bookstores and distributors worldwide.

They can also be obtained through online retail partners such as Amazon or by contacting the author on the address below.

Contacts:

21-23 Stokescroft

Bristol BS1 3PY

United Kingdom

E-mail:

kkasali@yahoo.com

Ingram Content Group UK Ltd.
Milton Keynes UK
UKHW020920070623
423006UK00009B/88